The Life and Times of Ty Cobb

by Norm Coleman

DEDICATION

I dedicate this book to the four people I love the most. My son, Mark Coleman; his wife, Christine Adachi Coleman; my lovely grandson, Trevor; and my nephew Steve Grant who encouraged me from the start.

Also dedicated to Mr. David Dombrowski, CEO, President and General Manager of the Detroit Tigers, now with the Boston Red Sox; Wesley Fricks, Ty Cobb Historian and Executive Director of the Ty Cobb Museum in Royston, Georgia; and Deb Wong, my editor.

CONTENTS

ACKNOWLEDGMENTS

To the many people who have helped me... from the start of
the Ty Cobb one-man show... to this book.
Sorry if I left your name out.

Jeremy MacKinnon, who helped with editing and design of the
book. Patti Dyson, Steve Grant, Bob Loudin, Hal Bogner and
Kathy Watts, Leonard Coleman, Deb and Mike Wong, Dr. Eli
T. Ross, Brian Heminger, Suzanne Black, Clay Beatty, Cameron
Palmer, Trina and Pierre Beatty, Lyn April Statten, Jim
McAllister, Julie Ridgeway, Herschel Cobb Jr.,
Marlene Vogelsang.

To contact the artists:
Cover photo: Arthur K Miller - www.artofthegame.com
Cobb Portrait: Dick Perez - dickperez.com

INTRODUCTION

Cobb has long been recognized as one of the greatest players to ever play baseball. He was known for his complex personality and competitiveness. During the early years of baseball known as the Deadball Era, he was recognized as the King of Baseball.

He was the first player elected into the Hall of Fame in Cooperstown, New York in 1936.

In 1999, the Major League Baseball All-Century team was chosen by popular vote of the fans. Ty Cobb was one of ten outfielders chosen.

As a rookie for the Detroit Tigers, he won nine consecutive batting titles from 1907 to 1915 leading the Tigers to three straight World Series appearances. He won twelve batting titles over his career that ended in 1928 with the Philadelphia Athletics. No other player has ever equaled those records.

He hit over .400 three times, was a triple-crown winner in 1909. His lifetime batting average of .367 is the best in baseball. Ty's 892 lifetime stolen base record is 3rd best behind Rickey

Henderson and Lou Brock. He stole home 54 times without ever being thrown out.

Cobb's aggressive style of play dominated the game both at the plate and on the base paths. His scientific study of the game in which he kept detailed notes on every pitcher, catcher, infielder and outfielder enabled him to know the weaknesses of the opposition. He often bunted down the lines beating throws to first. He got many a hit on slow grounders because, "I ran to first like a mugger was chasing me with a sharp knife and I ran for my life," he said.

Ty's style of play depended on daring, strategy and outthinking the enemy, especially on the base paths. "He didn't outhit the opposition, he outthought them," a teammate said.

Raised in Royston, Georgia, Ty started playing baseball at fourteen for the local team in Royston. He was the star of the team that consisted of boys between sixteen and twenty-two.

In 1905, Ty spent a year with the Augusta Tourists. In late August, his contract was sold to the Detroit Tigers for $750. He hit .240 that year. It was the only year of a twenty-three year career he failed to hit .300.

Strong-willed and competitive, willing to succeed at any cost, Ty maintained his confidence, determination, and strong work ethic drove him to succeed. "I outworked and out-practiced everyone." he said.

He had to be the best, and that is what he became.

CHAPTER ONE
Who was Tyrus Raymond "The Georgia Peach" Cobb?

Cobb quotes:
"When I began playing the game, baseball was about as gentlemanly as a kick in the crotch."

Ty had a demanding father who was a teacher and a student of ancient European and American history. It was his father, William Herschel Cobb who named his son Tyrus, after the Lebanon city of Tyre that showed tremendous courage in repelling the armies of Alexander the Great.

During his twenty-four year career, Ty was an MVP and Triple-crown-winner in 1909. He won nine consecutive batting titles between 1907 and 1915, and twelve batting championships over his career. He hit over .400 three times, and was by far the greatest player in the early days of baseball, known as the "Deadball Era."

Cobb played for the Detroit Tigers from 1905 to 1926. His final two years were with the Philadelphia Athletics, 1927 and 1928.

Ty was strong-willed and competitive, with a will to succeed at any cost. Due to the hazing he received from his teammates in his rookie season in 1906, he became a loner, seemingly at war with the world.

Late in life when asked by Cobb biographer, Al Stump, why he fought so hard in baseball, Cobb explained, "I did it for my father... I knew he was watching me in heaven, and I never let him down."

Ty Cobb was known for his reliance on strategy, quick thinking, stealing bases and outthinking his opponents. Cobb, like a chess master, was always a step ahead of his adversaries; always doing the unexpected, especially running the bases. One of his teammates said, "He didn't outhit or outrun the opposition - he outthought them."

With all the records he set, and the fabulous statistics he accrued, this gives you a thin idea of how Cobb dominated the game for two decades. He could break open a close game by his daring, quickness of thought and feet. He lays down a perfectly placed bunt for a single, inching slowly away from first, then further and further, drawing throws to first, while distracting the pitcher. The pitcher goes into his delivery, and Cobb bolts in a flash to second, causing the catcher to hurry his throw, wide of second into the outfield, and Cobb winds up on third.

He fakes a false start off third again, and again screaming at the pitcher, "I'm coming home, I'm gonna steal it." He draws a few throws to third, and on the next wind-up, he hurtles toward home, and safely beats the pitchers throw. Home was Ty's favorite base to steal - he stole home 54 times without ever being thrown out.

Cobb always tried at every opportunity to gain an advantage or an edge over his rivals. He played head games with his opponents. That is why he never denied spiking infielders and catchers, because he wanted them to think that that is what he would do, as he slid in.

He believed the dirt was about ten to fifteen feet before the base was his Ground - his "patch," as he called it. If an infielder was in his patch, trying to block him, he might get cut as he slid in, "…and it would be their fault." he said.

This painting of Mr. Cobb was done by Dick Perez, one of America's foremost artists of famous baseball players. Contact Mr. Perez - dickperez.com

Ty maintained that what made him great was his overpowering desire to be the best. It was the internal fire in his belly that drove him to practice harder and more than anyone, to be the best he could be. He would practice sliding until his legs were raw. He placed blankets down the baselines and practiced bunting the ball until it hit the blanket, giving him the edge to make it to first before the fielder could get the ball and fire to first, a second after Ty hit the bag.

Ty loved hunting in the off-season, and would tie weights to his legs so they would be strong in the upcoming season. He did everything he could to give him an edge over his opponents. Most of them loathed Ty, but admired his drive to be the best and to succeed.

Cobb continued to excel on the field throughout his career, clearly becoming the game's dominant player, and in the opinion of most of his contemporaries, he was the greatest player in baseball history.

He knew every president from William Howard Taft to Dwight D. Eisenhower.

Ty retired over eighty-five years ago, but he is the all-time leader in BAV with .367, second in runs scored, hits and triples, third in stolen bases behind Ricky Henderson and Lou Brock.

Cobb's record of 4191 hits remained on the books until Pete Rose, Cincinnati Red, passed Ty Cobb as career hits leader with No. 4,192 on Sept. 11, 1985, and finished his career with 4,256 hits.

His finest season was 1911 leading the American League in ten offensive categories. He hit .420, stole 83 bases, hit 47 doubles, 24 triples, scored 147 runs, had 127 runs batted in and a hitting streak of 40 games. His 40-game hitting streak enabled him to edge "Shoeless Joe Jackson" for the batting title.

Ty won the first MVP - then called the Chalmers Award - and was awarded a Chalmers car - at that time, the most exquisite car ever made in America. Cobb struck out swinging just two times that year.

Cobb won this luxurious Chalmers "30" car valued at $2,700 by winning the batting title in 1911 with a .420 average

His slugging percentage was 621 with 8 home runs, tied for second place, behind Frank Baker's 11.

Over his lifetime career, he stole home 54 times without ever being thrown out. Five times he stole second, third and home in the same inning. Once, he stole those three bases on three pitched balls.

Cobb was known for his reckless running and blinding speed. In a game against the New York Highlanders (later to become the New York Yankees), he scored from first base on a single to right field.

In another game that year, he scored from second on a wild pitch. In the same game, he hit a double, driving in two runs. On a close play at home, the umpire called the runner safe in a close play.

The Highlanders catcher argued loudly and long with the umpire. The infielders gathered around home plate to watch the proceedings.

Cobb realized no one had called time, casually strolled toward third base, and in a free and easy way, walked toward home plate as though he wanted a better view of the proceedings. He then suddenly slid into home, to score the game's winning run.

Although he could cause pain to infielders and catchers with his aggressive sliding, he could also cause pain to himself. Famed sportswriter and friend Grantland Rice wrote about a game Ty played: "Several games with each leg a mass of raw flesh, and a temperature of 103, caused doctors to urge him to take a few days off, so he could heal. Ty ignored doctors' orders and on that day, when he got three hits, stole three bases and won the game. After the game, he collapsed on the bench."

Many stories have been told about Cobb, some true, some not.

Ty once told a sports writer, "When the legend becomes fact, print the legend."[1]

Cobb's Early Life, Growing Up in Georgia

Ty (The Georgia Peach) Cobb was born in the Narrows, Georgia, on December 18, 1886, twenty-three years after the end of the Civil War (or the War Between the States, as the Southerners called it). He was born in The Narrows, Georgia

---

[1] In the film "The Man Who Shot Liberty Valance" Jimmy Stewart plays a man that goes on to fame and notoriety after everyone thinks he shot the notorious villain Liberty Valance. John Wayne's character was the one that in fact shot the criminal, but he let Stewart's character take the credit. When Stewart tries to tell the truth to a reporter, he is told, *"When the legend becomes fact... print the legend."*

but raised in Royston, Georgia, located about seventy-five miles northeast of Atlanta.

Ty Cobb's father, William Herschel Cobb was born on February 23, 1863. His mother, Amanda Chitwood was born on February 15, 1871. Wm Herschel Cobb, a rural schoolteacher, married Amanda on February 11, 1886. He was twenty-three, she was fifteen. It was very common in the South after the war for women to marry young.

Mr. Cobb was an educated and brilliant man; he was a student of American and ancient European history. He was a farmer, church deacon, mayor, newspaper editor, philosopher, scholar, state senator and teacher.

Tyrus Raymond Cobb was their first child, followed by brother, John Paul, born on February 23, 1889. Cobb's sister, Florence Leslie was born October 29, 1892.

Young boys did a lot of fighting in those days, and they still do. It was expected that boys fight "like a man." Ty came into the world with a combative, or "viral nature" as he described it, and had more than his share of contentious struggles.

Ty became fascinated with baseball at the age of six, and was often seen playing a game called "Cat." A player would throw a ball into the air, and the batter would swing, then run to first base. The fielder would then throw the ball as hard as he could at the runner. This resulted in many bruises that Ty would incur, but he learned to handle pain without crying. As Tom Hanks said in the film: "A League of their Own": *"There's no crying in baseball."*[2]

---

[2] America's stock of athletic young men was depleted during World War I professional all-female baseball league springs up in the Midwest. Sentimental and light, but still thoroughly charming, "A League of Their Own" is buoyed by solid performances from a wonderful cast: Tom Hanks, Geena Davis, Madonna and more.

A neighborly carpenter created the black ash bats that Ty played baseball with as a youngster. Ty was very proud of his bats and took them to Augusta and then to Detroit

Ty's mother Amanda Chitwood Cobb made his first glove, as well as his first uniform. Ty and his friends were often seen searching for scrap metal that he sold to buy his first mitt. Amanda noticed many times Ty throwing rocks into the air and hitting them with a branch. He would throw a ball against a wall, and practiced fielding for hours.

Ty joined a local team called the Royston Rompers that consisted of boys aged fifteen to twenty. Ty was twelve. He said, "I started playing series baseball at fourteen, and despite being short at 5'7" and weighing only 145 pounds soaking wet, I became the star of that team."

Ty's Youth in Georgia

Ty was twelve years old in junior high school when he engaged in a spelling bee, with boys against the girls. The girls won, and Ty was so angry at losing that he beat up a friend for misspelling a word. His dad punished him, making him work extra hard on the farm. "I couldn't play baseball for a week," Ty moaned. "I never did like losing, and second place didn't interest me," he said.

Mr. Cobb was well aware of Ty's anger and temperament. He wrote Ty a letter when he was fifteen. The letter said, "Be good and dutiful. Conquer anger and wild passions that would belittle your manhood. Cherish all the good that springs up in you. Be under the guidance of the better angel of your nature. Drive out the demon that lurks in all human blood and is ready, anxious, and restless, to arise and reign. Be good."[3]

---

[3] Richard Bak, *Peach: Ty Cobb in His Time and Ours* (Michigan: Sports Media Group, 2005).

Ty lived an idyllic childhood in Royston. He fished, hunted birds and squirrels and learned to swim in a local pool, helped by one of the colored men who worked on Mr. Cobb's farm.

He spent weeks at his grandfather's home. Grandpa regaled him with stories of how he battled the Yankees during the War Between the States. Ty was 7 years old then, and was thrilled to hear his stories.

"Grandpa told me we were going to hunt bear today, do you own a knife?" Gramps asked me," Ty said.

"No grandpa, but I own a slingshot." Ty told him.

"One day Ty, this big old bear surprised me. He stood up on his hind legs ... why, he was about fifteen feet tall, with monstrous claws and fangs as big as corncobs glistening in the brilliant sunlight. Saliva was pouring out of his mouth, and he was growling so loud I had to cover my ears. His breath alone nearly knocked me off my feet," grandpa said, with a twinkle in his eye. "And me armed only with a long rifle," he said.

Ty's eyes were huge as he listened intently, his eyes ablaze with excitement as he listened to grandpa's story.

"What happened, Grandpa, what happened?" Ty asked.

Grandpa lit his pipe, slowly looked Ty in the eye and said, "Ty, if I had missed, you wouldn't be here today."

Ty said, "My daddy and grandpa were the only men in my life who I loved and respected. They gave me their love and wanted nothing more from me than to be the best I could be. I vowed to do just that."

"My grandfather had a sense of wit and charm," Herschel Cobb Jr., told me after one of the shows in which he saw me perform.

As a child, Ty liked nothing more than to throw a hand-made baseball against a wall, and practiced fielding. In the hot and humid summers in Georgia, he played baseball from dawn to dusk, or until it got too dark to see, his mother Amanda reported.

He played town ball with friends and fell in love with baseball at an early age. He performed odd jobs for neighbors and used his money to buy a mitt. Ty was small at ten, but played ball on any team he could, whether they wanted him or not.

The Peach attended his first spring training in Augusta, Georgia in 1904. During the off-season, he was busy hunting, running and practicing his bunting techniques. He also became the baseball coach for a local prep school.

He was in superb condition and had grown to 6'1, 180 pounds when he reported at Warren Park, in Augusta for spring training in 1905. It was at this time that a writer from the Detroit Free Press reported about the boy wonder Tyrus Cobb, and gave him his nickname: "The Georgia Peach," named after the fabulous peaches grown in Georgia. He maintained that name for the rest of his life.

Ty set a standard for himself when staying in shape during the off-season by working out, running, not smoking, drinking beer, over-eating, reading books to rest his eyes, and getting lots of rest. He knew he had to develop the mental toughness to endure not only the long season ahead, but also the hazing his teammates would give him. He demanded of himself that he be the very best he could be, to make his deceased father proud of him.

Ty's Relationship with his Daddy

William Herschel Cobb, Ty's father was a highly respected man in and around Royston, Georgia. He was esteemed as a teacher, hired by the well-to-do to privately teach their children.

Mr. Cobb was well read, and had a library in their home with books on subjects such as American history, ancient European history, Middle Eastern history and novels by famous authors (Mark Twain, Charles Dickens, Herman Melville, Walt Whitman and many others) and the family bible. The young Ty devoured those books, and many more. Tyrus read many of the books in the library, but was not interested in school. Baseball was always on his mind. Mr. Cobb was a farmer, church deacon, mayor, newspaper editor, philosopher, scholar and state senator. Ty adored his daddy, saying, "I worshipped the ground he walked on - he was God, as far as I was concerned - he was a saint."

Herschel Cobb was appalled when he learned about the lynching of Negroes, and spoke out against that tactic. As a state senator, he talked about the value of education saying, "We tried slavery and serfdom to utter failure. It is educating our negro youth that will improve our culture."

Mr. Cobb let it be known about his plans to run for Governor of Georgia, but when he openly spoke his belief in the state legislature that Negroes should have the right to vote and own property, many people turned against him. The country was not ready for integration at that time. It was not until the Civil Rights Act was enacted into law in 1965 by President Lyndon B. Johnson that life began to change for African Americans.

Herschel also expressed his fondness for the late president Abraham Lincoln. Needless to say, that kind of thinking did not sit well with the voters of Georgia, thus dooming his plans for the Governorship.

His plans for his son were to attend West Point or the University of Georgia. Ty had his own plans, and totally disagreed with his revered father.

As was done in those days, Ty approached his daddy and asked for his blessings to play baseball with the Augusta Tourists, a team in the newly formed South Atlantic League.

Ty worked on the fifty-acre farm Mr. Cobb bought in Royston, Georgia, to supplement his income. "I developed a close relationship with my daddy. I grew strong working on the farm and played baseball whenever I could." Ty said.

"I worshipped the ground he walked on," Ty would say about his daddy. "Thanks to my daddy, I became one of the greatest players that ever played baseball."

Mr. Cobb did not want his son to play baseball. He strongly urged Ty to become a doctor, or a lawyer, an engineer, a military man or even a politician, like himself. Ty objected to his father's desire for him.

Ty exclaimed how much he loved playing baseball, and how good he was at the game. "I told my daddy I was going to make him be proud of me," Ty said.

Worn down by Ty's pleading, Herschel gave in and told his son to play baseball, "Get it out of your system," he said. "Don't come home a failure boy, don't you dare come home a failure. You be the best at whatever you do, if you want to be a ballplayer, you be the best that ever played the game."

And that is what Ty became, the very best. But Herschel never saw Ty play.

"The Georgia Peach" was quick to anger, and had numerous fights with black men and whites. He was aggressive on the field, but he played by the rules and did not intentionally spike infielders or catchers, as Al Stump reported.

As an adult, Ty was said to have a rotten disposition off the field. He was rude and crude, obnoxious, vindictive and lacking in any normal virtues. This is what some players believed, some sports writers wrote and many fans in those days and even today believe. The truth of the matter is while Cobb did have some issues most of the attributes given to Ty are false.

Cobb batting tips: Take your position at the plate, near the back line of batting box against right-handed pitchers, especially if he has a real curve. Try to hit to right-center and practice hitting right-handers to the opposite field. An inside ball from a right-hand pitcher you will naturally pull to left-center.

Did you know? Ty Cobb became the first Pro-Athlete to appear in a Hollywood movie when he starred in "Somewhere in Georgia" in 1917.

CHAPTER TWO
Cobb Reports to Augusta, Georgia

Cobb quotes:
"Baseball was one-hundred percent of my life."

The young Tyrus Raymond (The Georgia Peach) Cobb was a nineteen-year-old boy, tall, slender, muscular and full of himself when he reported to the Augusta Tourists for spring training in 1904.

He told anyone who would listen that his daddy, whom he dearly loved and had a close relationship with, would come to watch him play on opening day. He was positive he would play that day. He did not play; his father did not attend, and never saw Ty play.[4]

Cobb was the Pete Rose of his day, racing to his position in the outfield, running at top speed to the dugout, running, not walking to first on a walk. He foolishly attempted to extend singles to doubles and doubles to triples, sometimes succeeding, but mostly failing, much to the dismay of his manager and coaches. He bragged about being a natural born showoff.

---

[4] Charles Alexander, *Ty Cobb* (Dallas: Southern Methodist University Press) 1984.

"I had to be first and the best at everything I do," Ty maintained, while his teammates and coaches laughed at him.

This did not endear him to his teammates, nor did that attitude allow him to make many friends when he grew older. But it was that inner drive, his demand to be the best that enabled him to become the great player he eventually became.

He was always intent on showing off the potential greatness he believed was in him. He believed that thought, in his mind, heart, body and soul. And damn the enemies this caused him to make. Although he never said that he was going to be the greatest player that ever played the game, he strongly believed he would, knowing how proud this would make his father.

Early on, Ty displayed his willful disobedience or rebelliousness to authority. He wanted to play the game his way. It was that attitude that separated him from his opponents. Like Frank Sinatra, he did it his way. Later, as he matured, he claimed and stated that as a matter of fact, he out-worked and out-practiced everyone.

In Augusta during spring training in 1905, Cobb, in his own unique but immature way, was attempting to say: "Look at me - you have never seen anything like me, and never will!"

Though all of Cobb's shenanigans were annoying to Augusta Tourist management, they saw in him the potential to be a great baseball player. Management did not cut him after his poor 1904 season. He was brought back to Augusta the following year, and after a slow start, he met the coach that would change his life, George Leidy.

Later in the spring, Ty started a postal card-writing spree to Grantland Rice, a sports columnist for the Atlanta Journal known for his elegant prose. His writing was published in newspapers around the country and broadcast on the radio. Cobb was writing that a star player was playing in Augusta for the Tourists.

Cobb mailed over a hundred cards to Rice, all exclaiming the fans' love for the outstanding young star. Some cards were signed in pencil, others in ink. All were signed with false names like Brown, Smith and Jones, and all mailed from different towns, when Ty was on the road.

Cobb and Rice became great friends later, and Rice recalled receiving the cards from Ty. He placed an item in one of his columns saying: "A young star in Augusta named Ty Cobb is tearing up the Sally League, and is on his way to Detroit."

Modern sportswriters would say that enormously successful athletes like Cobb, Babe Ruth, Muhammad Ali, Joe Montana, Wayne Gretsky, Tom Brady, Tiger Woods and Michael Jordan all had the souls of champions, born with genes and DNA that would cause them to work and practice harder than other men, with a powerful belief that greatness was inside them.

A coach once told Ty he was a natural-born hitter. Cobb believed him, until he came to the conclusion there is no such thing. Just as there are no natural-born dancers, pianist, violin players or singers, it takes practice, practice, practice that would allow them to rise to the top.

Cobb would encounter bullying and hazing in his first season with the Tigers in 1906, and would have to deal with the murder of his father by his mother, Amanda Chitwood.

Ty would return to Augusta the following year and would have a fine season. He could not have known when the season started he was on his way to Detroit.

"Genius in Spikes"

Ty believed baseball is a game of the mind, as well as the body, brains as well as brawn. He called it a game of inches. He said, "I once heard Yogi Berra say that: "Baseball is 90% mental and 50% physical."

"I wasn't the fastest guy in the league; lots of guys were faster than me, but I was the smarter," Ty maintained.

"I knew the strength and weaknesses of every catcher as well as the pick-off attempts by every pitcher." Cobb declared.

Grantland Rice, a famous sports writer and friend of Ty called Cobb a "Genius in spikes" due to his approach to playing baseball: with his mind, his body and his feet. He saw the game as a science, keeping detailed notes on opposing pitchers and catchers. He knew their arms as well as his own. He studied the infielders and outfielders. He knew their weaknesses and strengths, keeping detailed notes in his notebook.

He used a stopwatch to clock the time it took for a pitch to arrive in the catcher's glove, and the time it took the catcher to throw to second base.

"If it took 3.5 seconds, and I could make it from first to second in 3.4, I'd be safe four out of five times, and I was rarely thrown out." he said. He was once clocked running from home to first in 3.1 seconds.

Cobb led the league in stolen bases 6 times, had 96 in 1915 and 892 lifetime. He stole home 54 times without ever being thrown out. These are records that lasted over sixty years.

"He was a cross between a tidal wave, cyclone, earthquake-fire, wind and water. Then out of the air comes the glitter of steel, plus ten tons of dynamite hitched to a spark." - Grantland Rice

Five times over his career, he stole second, third and home in the same inning. One time he did it on three consecutive pitches.

The Peach once hit a home run on a ground ball back to the pitcher. The throw to first was wild, and Ty wound up on third. He took a wide turn, daring the first baseman to pick him off. He took the cut-off throw from the right fielder, and believing he would catch Ty half way down the line, threw wild to third allowing Ty to score. The scorekeeper recorded it as a home run.

Murder in the Family

Cobb was enjoying a successful season with the Augusta Tourists, a minor league team in Georgia, when his contract was sold to the Detroit Tigers for $750.00. He was told to report to Detroit in a few days.

He wanted nothing more than to share this momentous occasion with his daddy, whom he worshipped and adored. His daddy was God as far as Ty was concerned. Unfortunately, this did not occur.

He was never so happy in his life, as all that he worked for and dreamed about was about to come to fruition. Ty invited his younger brother Paul and some of his friends to watch him play his last game for the Augusta Tourists. It was mid-August, 1905. His contract had been sold to the Detroit Tigers for $750.00, and he was to report to Detroit in three days. He was amazed at the amount of the sale. He said: "I couldn't believe I was worth so much money."

His devoted fans gave him a solid gold watch in appreciation for his excellent season. A beautiful young woman presented him with a dozen red roses.

But Ty went from the height of happiness to the depths of depression when he received the horrible news of the death of his beloved daddy.

When he learned the truth of how his father died, and the tragic way in which he met his death, this destroyed him. He said, "I never recovered and never got over the tragic death of my beloved daddy."

Ty reported to Detroit a few days later, but returned to Augusta to console his disconsolate mother, and got hits in his first two at-bats, showing his powerful sense of concentration.

Cobb Disappears from Tigers for Two Months

Rumors were rampant in the small town of Royston that Mrs. Cobb had had a lover. When Mr. Cobb heard the rumors, he told his wife that he was leaving town on business. He returned to their home later in the evening to catch Amanda in the act of making love with her lover.

When Amanda heard a noise outside of her bedroom late at night, she reached for her pistol to protect herself. Like many women in those days, she was a good shot. Mr. Cobb always kept a loaded pistol in a drawer in their bedroom. She fired her pistol twice, killing Mr. Cobb instantly.

Seven months after this unfortunate tragedy, Amanda Chitwood went to trial in Royston, for killing her husband. She was charged with 2nd degree manslaughter. Ty was deeply disturbed at the death of his beloved daddy. During the entire trial, Ty sat beside his mother, holding her soft, sweet hand. Despite the prosecution's attempt to find Mrs. Cobb guilty, an all-male jury acquitted her. Ty loved his mother, and never turned against her. She passed away in 1936.

In addition to this experience, Ty experienced a year of hazing and bullying from his teammates. That was common in those early days of baseball. Ty fought back, earning him an undeserved reputation that he always fought with his teammates. His failure to be accepted by his mates and the death of his father caused him to fall into a deep state of melancholia.

It was during the season of 1906 that Ty disappeared from Detroit in mid-July, causing him to miss a shade over 50 games.

It was thought at first he suffered from "stomach trouble." Later, doctors reported it was not a hernia. The Tigers front office did not communicate to the press, leaving the media to circulate rumors concerning Cobb's health.

Charles C. Alexander in his book claimed that Cobb suffered from "...some sort of emotional and physical collapse," but provided no additional information.

Ty was on the edge of a nervous breakdown as a result of the death of his father, and from the mental abuse he suffered from his mates. He was showing signs of instability; his nervous system was breaking down.

Given his apparent nervous breakdown, the Tiger media did not report to the public that Ty was sent to a sanitarium in rural upstate Michigan for a period of rest and relaxation.

He was given medication and had long resting periods of sleep, relaxation, and plenty of time to rest his anxious mind and body. He swam, fished and took long hikes in the nearby forest. He was not allowed to read newspapers, and the press was forbidden.

The Sanitarium was located in Pontiac, Michigan, and was leveled in 1972.[5]

Reports circulated in the Detroit Free Press that Cobb was resting at a home in the Northern part of Michigan, and doctors there said that he would be released before the end of the season.

Ty returned to the team in early September, his personality back, his eyes and skin bright, thanks to the salubrious air, sun and rest he had during his period away from the team.

---

[5] Sanitarium in those days was an establishment for the medical treatment of people who were convalescing from a chronic illness. Some people today refer to it as a "nuthouse."

He wound up the season with a .316 batting average. He never discussed his disappearance with teammates, the press, in any books he wrote, or were written about him. It was as though the shame of that experience was too difficult for him to ever discuss.

During the remaining twenty-three years of his career, he never batted less than .300, and hit over .400 three times. He was the first player elected into the Hall of Fame in Cooperstown, New York in 1936.

George Leidy, Mentor

Ty had a lot to learn about playing baseball, learning the finer points of the game, and growing up. At this time George Leidy, a clever, crafty and intelligent baseball man came into Ty's life. Leidy was a player-manager for the Augusta Tourists when Cobb arrived. He coached Ty and gave him a pep talk describing the luxury of the major leagues, exhorting Ty to stop fooling around and make the most of his ability.

George became his mentor and changed his life. Leidy was a part-time player and coach for the Augusta Tourists, with years of playing minor league ball.

He saw in the young Ty a star in the making. During morning practices, he taught the boy the hit and run, hitting to the opposite field, and the art of bunting. He threw practice balls at Ty for hours while he practiced bunting, drag bunts, faking bunts to third, and then slapping the ball past an incoming third baseman.

He would place a sweater down the first and third baselines, forty feet from home plate, and have Ty practice bunting to the sweater. He told Ty: "… by the time the pitcher or infielder got to the ball, you will be past first base."

Ty practiced sliding, and George taught him the fundamentals of the fade-away slide that Cobb mastered, sliding around the base, giving a fielder only the tip of his shoe to tag, sometimes sliding to the right of the bag, sometimes to the left.

If he noticed the fielders coming in expecting a bunt, he would have Ty pop the ball over their heads or drive the ball past them for a single or double. He convinced Ty to always be aware of where the infielders played. "Be aware, be alert, pay attention at all times" George stressed over and over to young Ty.

George never attempted to change the "hands apart" way that Ty held the bat, even though most players choked up. George believed Ty's magical way of moving his hands up or down the bat, depending upon how the pitch was thrown would bring him great results in the future.

Ty started his approach to holding the bat with hands apart when he was fourteen playing in Royston, Georgia, and he never changed to the choke- up approach. He always maintained that is why he was able to earn a .367-lifetime average.

Ty said, "By moving my hands up or down, I had great bat control to slap the ball to left, or punch it center or right. It made it easier for me to hit the ball between the fielders, just the way Wee Willie Keeler did."[6]

Cobb adopted Keeler's approach to "hit the pitch you can hit good, wait for that pitch, than hit 'em where they ain't."

---

[6] William (Wee Willie) Keeler played from 1891 to 1910 in the National League. He created the phrase, "hit 'em where they ain't!"

Leidy painted a picture in Ty's mind of what life would be like when he reached the majors. He said, "You will stay in fine hotels in the Northern cities, dress well, you will dine in fine restaurants, eat the best food, women will flock to you, businessmen will offer you gifts to be near you. And you will be paid well by the team owners."

Leidy stressed, "In order for that to happen, you must practice, practice, practice and want it, desire it, see it in your mind, and the celebrity that comes with it." Ty bought the picture hook, line and sinker, and that is what happened.

Years later, Cobb would say of Leidy, "Every young man who wants to play baseball should be as fortunate as I was to have a mentor, coach, a wise and patient man who took a young irresponsible boy, who thought he knew it all, and turned him into a man."

The Tourists won the opening day game that year against the Charleston Sea Gulls 2-1. Cobb had an inauspicious day at the plate having no hits in four at bats. He played errorless ball in left field. By the end of the year, 2005, Ty would be in Detroit.

Quotes about Cobb: "Ty Cobb lived off the field as though he wished to live forever. He lived on the field as though it was his last day." - Branch Rickey, GM, Brooklyn Dodgers

Cobb batting tips: "Don't grip your bat at the very end; leave say an inch or two. Also leave about an inch or more between your hands - that gives you balance and control of the bat. It also keeps your hands from interfering with each other during your swing."

Take your position at the plate, near the back line of batting box against right-handed pitchers, especially if he has a real curve. Try to hit to right-center and practice hitting right-handers to the opposite field. An inside ball from a right-hand pitcher you will naturally pull to left-center.

Cobb statistical record: Runs scored – 2245 (2nd all time)

CHAPTER THREE
Major League Debut

Cobb quotes:
"Every great hitter works on the theory that the pitcher is more afraid of him than he is of the pitcher."

Ty Cobb made his Major League debut on August 30, 1905 at the Polo Grounds in New York City. Yankee Stadium hadn't been built yet. He faced 41-game winner Jack Chesbro of the New York Highlanders. John D. Chesbro, nicknamed "Happy Jack," pitched for the New York Highlanders between 1903-1909. His 41 wins during the 1904 season remains a Major League record.

Chesbro also pitched for the Pittsburgh Pirates and Boston Red Sox. Later on, the New York Highlanders became the New York Yankees and Chesbro entered the Hall of Fame in 1946.

Cobb strolled into the on deck circle with three bats on his shoulder. No one had ever done that before. He believed that by carrying three bats instead of one, as most players did, it would create a sense of fear in the pitcher's mind, to frighten the pitcher. His teammates called him a hotdog, a baseball term for a show off.

Ty believed that when you drop the two heavy bats, the remaining one is light as a feather making it easy to swing. He was always thinking of little things like that to give him an edge. He strongly believed in getting into the heads of his opponents, to create doubt and fear in his opponents minds.

Chesbro had developed a reputation for being a nasty fastball pitcher, famed for his use of the spitball. A spitball is a pitch made with a ball moistened with saliva or any other liquid substance to make it move erratically. The pitcher might scratch the ball with a nail or his belt buckle, all this making it difficult for batters to hit.

Chesbro would throw the first pitch at a batter's head, especially if he was a rookie, as Ty was. Jack was a master at intimidation.

While the spitball was outlawed by Major League baseball in 1920, it was a legal pitch at that time. The pitcher spits on the ball, rubs it up real good and gets it all wet and slippery. He then fires it at the hitter at ninety miles an hour. The ball flutters and flies like a drunken butterfly on the way to the plate, making it hard to hit. The majors banned it in the early twenties.

Ty stepped into the batter's box brimming with confidence. Chesbro's first pitch was a fastball at his head, knocking him down. Ty said, "I heard him yell: "Welcome to the Big Leagues, boy!" Jack "...laughed his head off nearly falling off the mound," Ty said.

Chesbro yelled at Ty, "Hey Ty, I hear you're from the South, where men are men, and the sheep had better look out." Jack laughed so hard he fell of the mound.

In those days, players enjoyed dissing each other. Chesbro was one of the best. Cobb gave, as good as he got.

The young rookie got up, dusted himself off, and stepped back into the batter's box, digging in closer to the plate. He had no fear. "I never feared anything or anyone; you can't play baseball if you're afraid of getting hit by the pitch," Cobb maintained. The two opponents, one a highly respected veteran, the other a brash rookie started screaming at each other.

Ty yelled at him. "Is that the best you can do boy? My sister throws faster than you." He stared Chesbro down. He had no respect for the crafty enemy. He banged his bat on the plate, stepped out of the batter's box, and then slowly entered it in an attempt to throw Chesbro off his stride. Chesbro fired his second pitch up high and in tight, pushing him back. Jack was a master at intimidation.

The Peach banged his next pitch over the center fielder's head against the fence for a double. He took a long lead off the base and screamed at Jack, "I ain't afraid of you or any other pitcher in this damn league," Cobb roared loudly.

Cobb made a statement that day and kept it up for the next twenty-three years.

Detroit Baseball is Born

Baseball started in Detroit at the "Corner" on the streets of Michigan Avenue and Trumball Avenue. The park was called Bennett Park, and was located on land that was covered with oak and elm trees.

The year was 1901 and seven other teams joined the Tigers: The Boston Red Sox, Chicago White Sox, Cleveland Naps, New York Highlanders, Philadelphia Athletics, St. Louis Browns and

Washington Senators. A number of businessmen, seeing how much money owners of National League teams were making wanted in on what appeared to them to be a cash cow. The American League was born to compete against the powerful National League. The owners chose (Ban) Johnson as the first president of the league. Johnson, an executive in professional baseball, was born in Norwalk, Ohio and educated at Marietta College, Marietta, Ohio.

Frank Navin, a shrewd businessman, acted as general manager and baseball operations director for the Tigers. His decision in 1905 to buy the contract of a tall, skinny 18-year-old kid from Georgia named Tyrus Raymond Cobb from the Augusta Tourists for $750.00 set the stage for Detroit, and America to be introduced to a player that would make baseball America's National Pastime.

Cobb was regarded as brooding, reclusive and vicious. He was unknown to the fans and the media, and he took a brutal hazing from his uneducated veteran teammates. Cobb was a bible and book reading talented youngster from the South. His favorite authors were Charles Dickens, Herman Melville, Mark Twain and Walt Whitman.

He had a love of classical music that made matters worse for him. His favorite violinist was Fritz Kreisler. Friedrich "Fritz" Kreisler was an Austrian-born violinist and composer. One of the most noted violin masters of his or any other day, he was regarded as one of the greatest violin masters of all time. Cobb said, "I could listen to Fritz for hours.

Ty was a rebel! He played by the rules of the game, but broke none. He was an individual who played the game outside the box. He was the Picasso of the baseball world.[7] He used his

---

[7] Pablo Picasso was a Spanish painter, sculptor, printmaker, ceramicist, stage designer, poet and playwright who spent most of his adult life in France. He

mind to baffle his opponents, often making them look foolish, causing them to make mistakes. It is no wonder many opposing players disliked and even hated him.

Ty lacked the charm and outgoing personality of many of his teammates. He didn't smoke, drink, or use the foul language that many of his mates engaged in. He was not a jokester nor did he laugh at the silly jokes and pranks his teammates engaged in. Nor did he tell stories or pull pranks, as his teammates did.

Known for his speed and daring on the base paths, Ty was one of the fastest runners in the game, leading the league in stolen bases six times over his career.

Cobb in traditional pose with 3 bats on his shoulder.

changed the art world seeing and creating art his way.

If he had a character flaw, it was his inability to socially engage with the other players. This led some of the players to believe that Cobb felt himself to be smarter or better and above them. He was snooty and looked down his nose, some of his teammates maintained.

Cobb would deny this in the future, saying he always was a poor mixer socially, a loner, not because he wanted to be, but that was his basic nature. The fact that he was a Southerner while most of the Tigers were Northerners also played into his not being accepted by many of the players.

Tiger management knew what was going on in the clubhouse, but elected to close their eyes and minds on this matter, claiming it was natural, and that Cobb should "Ignore the hazing and get on with it," This Cobb could not do.

Ty was never hesitant to speak his mind. He told his teammates, "The idea of hazing young rookies was childish and detrimental to team unity."

When Ty spoke his mind his mates only poured it on more. Of course, he was right, but hazing rookies was part of the culture of baseball at that time, and still is today. But not to the extent it was done in Ty's days.

Cobb quickly introduced baseball to his way playing the game, which was intimidating other players with his cunning, brilliant style of running and stealing bases. His aggressiveness on the base paths and a hitting style different from other players would help him lead the Tigers to three straight World Series appearances, (1907-1909) and win nine consecutive batting titles, (1907-1915). This caused some of his teammates to be jealous of the talented, successful Ty.

On April 20, 1912, a new concrete and steel ballpark opened, holding over 26,000 fans, called Navin Field. On the same day in Boston, Fenway Park made its debut against the New York Highlanders.

Cobb rose to the occasion with a magical display of offense. He had two hits, scored two runs and stole home twice, his favorite base to steal. "My specialty," he called it. Eventually, he wound up with fifty-four steals of home, a record that still remains on the books.

He made two circus catches in the outfield and in the first inning with his teammate Sam Crawford, pulled off a double steal.

The Tigers beat the Cleveland Naps 6-5 in 11 innings.

Cleveland was called the Naps in honor of their star, Larry Napoleon Lajoie. Lajoie was a great hitter with a lifetime BAV of .338 and played for Cleveland and Philadelphia from 1900-1916. He was batting champion in 1901-1904 and elected into the Hall of Fame 1937. Eventually the park became known as Tiger Stadium. In January 1915, the name Naps was dropped, and Cleveland became the Indians.

Cobb retired at the end of the 1926 season, leaving the Tigers, but electing to sign with the Philadelphia Athletics managed by his friend Cornelius Alexander McGillicuddy (Connie Mack).[8] This was in hopes of restoring his reputation that was sullied by an accusation of gambling on baseball. The accusation was false. Commissioner Kenesaw Mountain Landis found Ty innocent of the charge.

---

[8] Cornelius Alexander McGillicuddy better known as Connie Mack, was a player, manager and team owner. The longest-serving manager in Major League Baseball history, he holds records for wins (3,731), losses (3,948), and games managed (7,755), with his victory total being almost 1,000 more than any other manager. Mack managed the Philadelphia Athletics for the club's first 50 seasons of play, starting in 1901, before retiring at age 87 following the 1950 season.

When the A's played the Tigers on Cobb Day in 1927, 30,000 fans came out to cheer and pay tribute to "The Greatest Tiger of Them All."

Ty retired after the 1928 season telling manager Connie Mack, "If a man can't hit better than .323, he should hang up his spikes and glove." And that is what he did.

Cobb's statue stood for years outside Comerica Park in Detroit and Turner Field in Atlanta, Georgia. It was moved in early 2017 to Royston, Georgia and now stands outside the Ty Cobb Museum.

Charles Comiskey, White Sox Owner

The owner of the Chicago White Sox was enamored by Ty Cobb and made several offers to the Tigers to buy his contract. It was always rejected.

The Tigers were not about to trade or sell Cobb's contract. Comiskey said, "I'd trade my right arm and offer Detroit any amount of money to buy his contract and bring him to Chicago." The Tigers were not about to trade or sell Cobb's contract.

Ty was aware of Comiskey's desire, but told Detroit reporters, "He never offered me the kind money I wanted. I knew he was one of the cheapest owners in the league. He was a two-bit miserly dime-store man. His cheapness in my opinion led to the 1919 scandal that induced his team to throw the World Series to Cincinnati." Ty said.

Despite Ty's comment in the Detroit Free Press, Comiskey said of Cobb, "He is the greatest player that ever played the game. He is dedicated and hard-driving with a fierce desire to win at any cost."

Charles also said, "Ty is a student of the game, willing to learn something about baseball every day of his life. He is the most intelligent ballplayer I have ever known"

When Ty read of Comiskey's remarks, he quipped to a reporter in Detroit, "I was always an admirer of Mr. Comiskey's insights and intelligence."

Cobb Quote: "Ted Williams is one batter I thought would break my lifetime batting average of .367. If he'd learned to hit left, Ted would have broken every record in the book!"

Cobb Quote: "Shoeless Joe Jackson's swing was purely natural… he was the perfect hitter. He never figured anything out or studied anything with the same scientific approach I gave it. He just swung hard. Joe Jackson hit the ball harder than any man I ever saw play baseball."

Cobb Statistics:

Most games with 5 or more hits – Lifetime	14
Most games with 5 or more hits – Season	4
Most games with 1 or more consecutive hits	40
Most games played – Lifetime	3033

CHAPTER FOUR
Cobb's Motto: "Pay Attention"

Cobb quotes:
"Shoeless Joe Jackson was the finest natural hitter in the history of the game. His .356 lifetime batting average is third best behind me and Rogers Hornsby."

Ty kept detailed notes on all his opponents. He kept a notebook and studied the catchers, pitchers and hitters. He studied their weaknesses and strengths. He wanted them to think about him. It was his idea of psychological warfare. Get into their heads, mess up their thinking. Although he never intentionally spiked infielders or catchers, he wanted them to think he would, giving him an advantage. Ty's motto was "Pay attention."

While his teammates were out drinking after a game, he would stay in his room, until late in the evening. He enjoyed listening to classical music playing softly in the background while he thought up ideas to beat his opponents and jotted them down in his notebook.

"When I am on the bases," Cobb said, "I try to get as close to home plate as I could. Feet and inches meant a lot to me."

Cobb stole home 54 times without ever being thrown out. One time in Detroit, he stole second, third and home on three consecutive pitches. He called it, "my favorite base to steal."

From the time Ty was a young lad growing up in Royston, Georgia, he dreamed of playing Major League baseball when he grew up.

He often had difficulty sleeping nights so he would get up and stroll around that sleepy little village. He'd walk all night, gazing up at the bright stars in the big, black, beautiful night sky, and dreamed of playing baseball in the Northern cities.

He pictured himself playing baseball in cities like New York, Brooklyn, Boston, Chicago, Cincinnati, Cleveland, Detroit, Philadelphia, Pittsburgh, St. Louis and Washington.

Ty had never been outside of Georgia until he arrived in Detroit in late August 1905. He heard many stories about what life was like in the Northern Cities. He was told there were many tall buildings, some as high as 30 or 40 stories. This was astounding to a boy growing up in a small village like Royston.

He read about the new ballparks being built in the North, parks that held thirty or forty thousand people. He heard they were paying players, three, four or five thousand dollars a year to play baseball and he wanted to be a part of that.

He was told about the big hotels and wonderful restaurants, museums and movie theaters with silent films coming out of Hollywood, and riding the fast moving trains from city to city. It sounded exciting to the young man coming to the small, quiet town of Royston.

He visualized himself playing in those Northern ballparks, and he always saw himself as a success.

"Ty was the only player that could score from third on a weak pop-up," Casey Stengel said.[9] "He would take a lead off third, and when the fielder flipped the ball to the pitcher, he would tag up and break for home."

Cobb's fame was spreading far and wide. His celebrity reached the White House. William Howard Taft was in the oval office. Taft, a huge golf and baseball fan would great Ty at the Park, shake his hand vigorously and remind Ty of their Augusta, Georgia connection. He was also a huge man weighing in at three hundred and fifteen pounds, the heaviest president in history.

In February 1960, seventeen months before he died, Ty gave a lucid interview to sports columnist Dan Daniel of the *New York World Telegram and Sun*.[10]

Cobb told Dan, "I played many games in New York. The fans heckled me but admired me as a player. I wasn't popular like Ruth was. I wasn't here to win a popularity contest. I came to whip the Yankees," Cobb remarked.

He also told him, "The fans razzed me hoping I would lose my focus, my concentration, but instead, it made me concentrate more and I worked harder to achieve my goal of

---

[9] Stengel was a Major League Baseball outfielder and manager. He managed the New York Yankees to five consecutive World Series Championships between 1949 and 1953. He was elected to the Baseball Hall of Fame in 1966.

[10] Dan Daniel was an American sportswriter whose contributions over a long period led him to be called the Dean of American Baseball Writers. He covered baseball in New York from 1910 through the 1960's. Mr. Daniel spent much of his career with the New York World Telegram and the New York World Telegram and Sun.

helping my team win. It didn't matter who liked me as long as I was revered for my accomplishments," Ty said.

The Peach ended the interview by exclaiming to Daniel, "I should get down on my hands and knees and thank the game for what it had done for me."

Walter Perry (The Big Train) Johnson, Hall-of-Fame Pitcher

Johnson, along with Cobb, Ruth, Honus Wagner and Christy Mathewson were elected into the Hall of Fame in the first class of players in 1936.

He won 417 games over a 21-year career and twice won over 30 games, all with the Washington Senators. Johnson holds the Major League record of 110 shutouts. He once won 16 consecutive games.

There were no radar guns to calculate the speed of Johnson's fastball. Cobb described them as hearing the sound the ball made on its path to the catcher's glove. And smelling the smoke made when the ball hit the bat.

In an interview Walter gave to a Washington sports writer, he said of Ty Cobb, "I'm glad to pay tribute to the greatest of all ballplayers, and to my esteemed friend. More than any man in the history of baseball, Ty Cobb has combined the arts of all aspects of the game, and used them with a really brilliant mind."

Cobb studied and made notes on every pitcher, including Johnson. The Big Train's first game in 1907 was against Cobb's Tigers in Washington, the Tigers won 3-2. Ty was held to one hit, a bunt single.

When the next batter bunted, his bold running found him on third where he scored on a fly ball. He also stole two bases in the game.[11]

Cobb & Walter Johnson: Johnson was one of the most feared pitchers in the league. Cobb had 120 hits in .328 AB's for an average of .366. Cobb's lifetime average was .367.

Walter was a tall right-handed pitcher who stood 6'2." He had a slingshot delivery with enormous speed and good control. Cobb was so impressed by Johnson that he urged Tiger management to "Sign this kid no matter what it costs. He has the best arm I ever saw, and he scared me."[12]

---

[11] Marc Okkonen, *The Ty Cobb Scrapbook: An Illustrated Chronology of Significant Dates in the 24-Year Career of the Fabled Georgia Peach* (New York: Sterling) 14
[12] Alexander, *Ty Cobb*, 101 -102.

Some reporters wrote that Johnson "owned" Ty but Cobb had 120 hits in 328 at bats or a .366 average, one point less than his lifetime average, .367.

Cobb realized the difficulty as good as he was that getting around on Walter's fastball was almost impossible. He concentrated on getting enough wood on the ball to slap it to left for a single or double.

Having studied Johnson well, Ty knew that Walter had a fear of beaning a player, even killing him if his fastball hit the batter's head. "Walter was a decent man," Cobb said. Thus, he proceeded to take advantage of Johnson's fear.

Ty often hung his head over the plate. Johnson, fearful of beaning Ty, pitched him low and away and outside giving Ty many walks.

Tris (The Grey Eagle) Speaker

Tris E. Speaker was considered one of the best offensive and defensive center fielders in baseball history. He was with the Boston Red Sox World Series winners in 1912 and 1915.

Speaker spent most of his career with the Boston Red Sox and Cleveland Indians, regularly hitting in the upper .300s and leading the league in doubles eight years. He played in the Deadball Era from 1907-1922 compiling a lifetime BAV of .345, 5th best in history.

Tris Speaker was considered one of the greatest center fielders of his day. He had 3515 hits, 5th best in history. He played for the Red Sox, Indians, Senators and Athletics. In 1920, he managed the Cleveland Indians to its first pennant and World Series victory over Brooklyn. He was voted into the Hall of Fame in 1937 one year after Cobb.

His 792 career doubles is the all-time best, Cobb was fourth with 724.

Tris had 3,514 hits, 5th best all-time.

Cobb had won nine consecutive batting titles from 1907 to 1915 coming into the 1916 season. Speaker hit .386 that year with Cleveland, and wrestled the crown from Cobb who slumped to .371

Cobb and Speaker were hunting and fishing buddies. The men enlisted several other players and dubbed them their "All Stars" and lit out for Canada, where they meant to mix business and pleasure.

They came to hunt, booking lodging at Rice Lake, Ontario, a lovely slice of Ontario cottage country. Along their way they scheduled a pair of exhibition games in Toronto. Ty Cobb and Tris Speaker were accused of gambling on baseball. (See chapter twelve for details.)

Cobb the Actor, in Theater and Movies

Cobb met many celebrities in the off-season including Jack Norworth, the composer of *"Take Me Out to the Ballgame"*[13]

He also met playwright George Ade who wrote *"The Seven Little Foys."* George offered Ty $10.000 to play a three month run as co-star in his play "The College Widow" Ty laughed it off saying, "I don't want to make a fool of myself acting on a stage."

When told he would be coached, Ty thought about the money and took the job playing a star All-American football

---

[13] Al Stump, *Cobb: A Biography* (Chapel Hill, NC: Algonquin Books) 1996

player.[14] The show opened in Trenton, New Jersey. A local theater critic said of his performance, "He ran around the stage a lot and scored several touchdowns." The audience enjoyed seeing Cobb on stage, and cheered loudly when he took his bows at show's end.

Cobb never gave thought to a career in the theater but brought the same intensity and spirit to the stage as he displayed on the diamond.

Ty was the first professional athlete to star in a Hollywood motion picture. At the end of the 1916 season, he starred in the film *"Somewhere in Georgia."* He played a small town bank clerk.[15]

The script was written by famed sports writer Grantland Rice, a friend of Ty's. Filmed in New York, Ty played a bank clerk who was yearning for his girlfriend and returns to Georgia to renew their friendship. He is kidnapped by villains but he escapes. Early in the film, he signed a contract to play for the Detroit Tigers. At the end of the film, he returns to Detroit and gets a hit to win the game for the Tigers.

A film critic called the movie, "The worst film ever made." Cobb never made another film, sticking to baseball instead.

Quotes about Cobb: "I never saw anyone like Ty Cobb. No one was even close to him as the greatest all-time ballplayer. The guy was superhuman, amazing." - Casey Stengel.

Cobb statistical records: 723 doubles (4th all time)

---

[14] Bak, *Peach*

[15] Tim Hornbaker, *War on the Basepaths: The Definitive Biography of Ty Cobb* (Champaign, IL: Sports Publishing) 2017.

CHAPTER FIVE
Cobb on Segregation

Cobb quotes:
"When I played ball I didn't play for fun. It's no pink tea, and mollycoddles had better stay out. It's a contest and everything that implies; it's a struggle for supremacy, a survival of the fittest."

Cobb did not speak openly about his feelings concerning segregation but he did not oppose racial segregation in baseball, given the times he lived in. His thoughts were neutral on the subject, despite his Georgia upbringing. Years later, he took a more liberal point of view, and spoke out about ending segregation in baseball.

Considered a racist by some, in 1952, in an article published by the Associated Press concerning the Texas League, the League had just become integrated, and Cobb came out in favor of integration.

He said, "Certainly it is O.K. for them to play. I see no reason in the world why we shouldn't compete with colored athletes, as long as they conduct themselves with politeness and gentility." Cobb believed segregation was a lousy rule.

Cobb separated himself from Southern racists like Dixie Walker and Enos Slaughter by his praise of Willie Mays, Jackie Robinson and famed Dodger catcher, Roy Campanella.

Fred "Dixie" Walker played on 3 Major League teams before arriving in Brooklyn where he played for the Dodgers from 1938-47. In 1947, he started a player strike due to his refusal to play with Jackie Robinson. He was traded to the Pirates at the end of the '47 season.

Enos "Country" Slaughter was born in Roxboro, North Carolina. He played for the St. Louis Cardinals from 1939 to 1953 when he joined the New York Yankees. He achieved fame by making a mad dash from first to home in the 1946 World Series, scoring the winning run against the Boston Red Sox.

Slaughter was one of the leaders of racial taunting against Jackie Robinson's first game in St. Louis. He injured Robinson inflicting a seven-inch gash on Robinson's leg with his spikes. Enos later denied any animosity toward Robinson.

Cobb traveled the Negro Leagues after his retirement, often sitting in the dugout with the players and once threw out the first pitch in a Negro League Park.

Cobb acquired the nickname "The Georgia Peach" by a reporter on the Detroit Free Press after the fabulous peaches grown in Georgia. He was universally recognized as the best player from the dead ball era.

He also had the reputation of being its most ferocious player. Cobb's fierce determination to succeed helped him to equal or surpass more offensive records than any other player, and his career average of .367 is still the highest of all time.

Cobb is pictured here with Brooklyn Dodgers pitcher Don Newcombe. Newcombe was the Dodger's starting pitcher for the first game of the 1949 World Series. With Cobb is nine-year-old Bruce Howard, a recovering polio victim who threw out the game's first pitch. The Dodgers lost the game 1-0.

He was a stalwart supporter of his team, with a strong desire to lead the team to the World Series. He accomplished that during the years 1907, '08 and '09 though the Tigers lost all three, twice to the Chicago Cubs in 1907-08 and once to the Pittsburgh Pirates in 1909.

Cobb's unyielding, often-ferocious work ethic and tenacious drive for success made him many enemies. His occasional episodes of violence ruined an otherwise impeccable career. He admitted he had a short fuse or a "viral nature."

The Wedding

It was late August 1905. Cobb was having a fine season with the Augusta Tourists when word got to him that his contract was sold to the Detroit Tigers for seven hundred and fifty dollars and he was to report to Detroit in three days. He said, "I couldn't believe I was worth so much money!"

In appreciation for the fine season he had, his devoted fans gave him a solid gold watch. A beautiful young woman presented him with a dozen roses. The charming young lady was Charlie Marion Lombard. She was from a prominent Augusta family.

Cobb said of Charlie, "She was a glamorous looking Southern Belle, with long flowing blond hair and skin as soft as a new born baby. Her blue eyes were brighter than the deep blue sky, brilliantly lit by the dazzling sun high above." Ty exclaimed.

"When she gently handed me the bright red roses, my heart beat faster than a Walter Johnson fastball. When she softly whispered in my ear, "Good luck in Detroit," the softness in her voice, made me blubber, "Thank you." Cobb said.

Ty exclaimed, "I fell in love with her the moment I laid eyes on her. I was in love for the first time in my life."

On August 8, 1908 they married at "The Oaks," the Victorian mansion home of her wealthy parents, Roswell and Nancy Lombard. The stately home was located nine miles from Augusta. Ty was twenty-one, Charlie was eighteen.

Charlie's father was a wealthy Augusta businessman who owned thousands of acres of rich farmland. Mr. Lombard made it very clear to his daughter how he felt about his beautiful young daughter marrying a young ballplayer, who was beneath her status in local society. Her daddy told Charlie he did not approve of the marriage, and would refuse to support her in the manner that she was raised. Ty would prove Mr. Lombard, wrong, very wrong.

Cobb supposedly had the consent of the Tigers manager to leave in mid-August to marry Charlie, causing rancor with his teammates for his leaving in the middle of a pennant race.

The local newspapers covered the wedding in both the sports and society pages reporting that the Southern gentleman Tyrus Raymond Cobb was marrying the socialite Southern lady, Charlie Marion Lombard. It was reported to be the greatest social event in Georgia history since the start of "The War Between the States" began in 1861.

Cobb Family Life

Ty and his wife Charlie had five children. The first was Tyrus Raymond Jr., born on January 30, 1910, followed by daughter Charlie Marion, June 2, 1911. Their 2nd son, Roswell Herschel was born on September 29, 1917. Beverly, September 19, 1919. Their last child, and 3rd son, James Howell was born on July 24, 1921.

Cobb may have lacked patience in dealing with many people, but he was affectionate with his children. However, as the children aged, Ty exhibited an unrealistic assumption as to how they should behave that created stress in the household.

Ty loved hunting dogs, show dogs and domestic dogs with many pets for the children to play with. When they got older, he bought horses for the children and taught them to ride.

Although Ty was a stickler for discipline, he never was physically abusive to his children. Neighbors reported seeing Ty play with his children and the neighbor's kids.

He joined the Masonic order of Masons at twenty-five and participated in many of the Shriners' charitable events.

Ty and Charlie were divorced in 1947, and in September 1949, Cobb married Florence Cass.

Roswell Herschel Cobb, 33, died of a heart attack in April 1951.

Tyrus Raymond Cobb Jr., 42, died of a brain tumor in September 1952.

Cobb was heartbroken as any parent would be at the loss of a child. His wife, Charlie Marion Lombard Cobb passed in February 1985. She was 84. I have had the good fortune to become friends with his grandchildren, Herschel Cobb Jr., and granddaughter Cindy Cobb. Both have seen the show.

Cindy thanked me for bringing the story of her grandfather to a current culture. Herschel commented on capturing the personality of grandpa as he knew him.

Quotes about Cobb: "Once on a golf course in Augusta, Georgia, I was about to put on the fifth green when I heard a voice yelling, 'Get out of my way, I'm coming through!' So I made way and Ty Cobb played right through me without apology. I guess nobody but the great Cobb would dare to do that to a president." - Dwight D. Eisenhower, 1964.

Cobb batting tips: "Keep your back leg straight. If you put your weight more on the front leg, the back leg will be straight."

Cobb statistical records: Cobb holds the record for most batting titles - 12.

CHAPTER SIX
Cobb Leads Tigers to Three Consecutive World Series

Cobb quotes:
"I have observed that baseball is not unlike a war, and when you come right down to it, we batters are the heavy artillery."

Ty Cobb won nine consecutive batting championships starting in 1907 when he hit .350. He won twelve batting championships over his career, another record he holds.

He led his Tigers to three straight World Series appearances. Unfortunately, they lost all three, twice to the dominating pitching and hitting of the Chicago Cubs in '07 and '08 and the Pittsburgh Pirates in 1909 led by future Hall of Famer Honus Wagner and a young Babe Adams who beat the Tigers three times.

The Series in 1907 was only the fourth in history, the first for the Detroit Tigers having won their first pennant. They found themselves against the pitching rich Chicago Cubs. The Cubs had won a record of 116 games the previous season, and 107 in 1907. The Tigers were just happy to be there.

The first game lasted twelve innings ending in a 3-3 tie. The game was called due to darkness. Tiger fans were disappointed in the team's poor showing, losing the next four games.

Cobb, in his first World Series hit a dismal .200 with 4 hits in 20 AB. He had a great season winning the batting title with a .350 BAV, 212 hits and stole 49 bases. As a sign of his blossoming fame, he signed a contract with Coca-Cola to promote Coke.

Cobb explained his poor hitting due to his inexperience in such a pressure packed environment. Great Chicago pitching stopped Ty in his tracks.

Just shy of his 21st birthday, he would be the youngest player to win a batting title until Al Kaline; also a Tiger beat him out by one day when he won the title in 1955. Al still holds that record.

Ty led the Tigers to three World Series: 1907-08-09

Cobb led the Tigers to their second consecutive World Series appearance in 1908 by winning his 2nd consecutive batting title hitting .324.

In a reprise of the previous year, the two teams met again in 1908, yet once again, the Cubs prevailed, beating the Tigers 4-1. This turned out to be the last time the Cubs would ever win a World Series, starting a losing streak that has lasted 107 years but ended in 2016 when the Cubs beat the Cleveland Indians, 4-3.

Cobb had a great game three going, 4 for 5, leading the Tigers to their only win, 8-3. He had a better series this time getting seven hits in nineteen at-bats hitting .368 with four RBI's.

Cobb won his third consecutive batting title with a .377 average, and led the Tigers to their third consecutive pennant and World Series appearance in 1909. They faced the powerful Pittsburgh Pirates, led by future Hall of Famer, shortstop, Honus Wagner. Ty would eventually win nine consecutive batting titles between 1907 and 1915, a major league record that remains on the books to this very day.[16]

He led the league in stolen bases with seventy-six, in hits with 216, in total bases with 296, in home runs with 9, and RBI with 107. He was however, unable to bring a championship to Detroit. The Pirates won the Series 4-3.

Once again, Ty could not break loose, and had a poor series having 6 hits with 26 AB and a BAV of .231. The hero of the series was a 27-year-old reserve pitcher named Babe Adams who beat the Tigers 3 times including a shutout in game seven.

---

[16] Multiple Batting Championships: Ty Cobb (12), Tony Gwynn (8), Honus Wagner (8), Rod Carew (7), Rogers Hornsby (7), Stan Musial (7), Ted Williams (6), Wade Boggs (5).

Cobb's statistics for the three World Series are: AB 65 H 17 SB 5 BAV .261.

Cobb became the first of many future Hall-of-Famers who also had a disappointing Series. Ty's BAV in 17 games was .261. Stan Musial, Ted Williams and Willie Mays also had dismal Series batting averages.[17]

Ty maintained his biggest disappointment in his baseball career was never winning the World Series.

The Tigers won their first World Series in 1935 beating the Chicago Cubs 4-2 managed by Mickey Cochran. Cobb attended several games. The Tigers beat the Cubs again in 1945, 4-3 and the St. Louis Cardinals in 1968 4-3 led by Mickey Lolich who won 3 games. Denny McLain (The last 30 game-winner) won game 6.

Five players on the Tigers have had their numbers retired including Cobb.[18]

Major-league baseball clubs didn't start putting numbers on uniforms until the 1930s. As a result, Cobb who played for the Tigers from 1905 to 1926 didn't have his uniform number retired because Cobb never was issued a number.

Ty attended many World Series but his favorite occurred in 1945 when his Tigers beat the Chicago Cubs 4-3 led by his good friend Hal Newhouser who won 2 games including game seven and Hank Greenberg who hit two homeruns. Both men eventually become Hall of Famers.

---

[17] Stan Musial, .256 in 23 games. Willie Mays, .239 in 20 games. Ted Williams .200 in his only Series. AB 25 H 5 BA .200.
[18] Al Kaline #6 -1980, Charlie Gehringer #2 1983, Hank Greenberg #5 1983, Hal Newhouser #16 -1997, Willie Horton #23 -2000.

Superstitions in Baseball

Ball players have been known to be superstitious, though most will not admit it. Many though believed in luck. Cobb was different, as he talked about his feelings on the subject.

Cobb said, "When I'm doing well, like when I am in a hitting streak,
I always do everything the same way. I go to the park via the same route, put on my uniform the same way and I hang up my towel on the same peg."

"As I ran in from center to the dugout, I superstitiously always stopped at second, touched the edge of the bag, then stepped on the base and continued to the dugout," he mentioned.

A reporter asked Ty if he ever slid into a base head first. He answered, "That's what I did the first time I tried to steal second in my first game as a Tiger. The shortstop slapped my head hard with his glove, stomped on my back and threw dirt into my eyes. I got up dizzy and bleeding all over. I heard the umpire yell, you're out."

"The best way to slide into any base is feet first," he continued. "Sliding head first was dumb and I never did that again," he said.

Cobb paid the price for his success. He would practice sliding until his legs were raw. During the winter, he hunted in weighted boots so his legs would be strong for the coming season.

He said, "I have more scars on my ankles, legs, thighs, shoulder and back and most of those spiking were unintended.

Francis Joseph (Lefty) O'Doul

Lefty O'Doul arrived in the Majors with the New York Yankees in 1919 as an inept pitcher. His record over four years was one win and one loss. He was so awful that he quit baseball for four years.

He surfaced with the New York Giants in 1928 when he met Ty Cobb during spring training. Cobb was a master at teaching hitting techniques and recognized the potential Lefty had. That year, he batted .319 but the following season, he led the National League in batting hitting .398. It was the highest average of any National League outfielder in the 20th century.

He also hit 32 home runs. Lefty retired with a lifetime average of .349 placing him in fourth place behind, Cobb, Rogers Hornsby and Shoeless Joe Jackson. Lefty was a San Francisco celebrity.

His restaurant bar in San Francisco simply called Lefty O'Doul's is world-renowned.[19] He always gave credit to Ty Cobb for enabling him to become the great hitter he became.

Lefty brought baseball to Japan in the early thirties, introducing many players such as Babe Ruth, Jimmy Foxx, Lou Gehrig, Connie Mack and many others to the Japanese people.

Cobb developed a reputation for being a shrewd investor and businessman and was always being asked to invest in this deal or that business. When O'Doul was planning to open his bar and restaurant in the theater district of San Francisco, he asked Cobb to partner with him. Ty politely declined the offer due to

---

[19] In November 2014, I performed my Cobb show at the request of the current manager of Lefty's Mr. Nick Bovis. This was an annual fundraiser for poor and neglected children of San Francisco. The restaurant is known for its wonderful buffet and massive amount of sports photos on the walls including one of Ty Cobb.

business reasons claiming, "Lefty drank more than I did, and I never did business with any man who could out-drink me."

Cobb and Lefty O'Doul

Lefty O'Doul was the one who told Cobb about the young Italian boy from San Francisco named Joe DiMaggio. The year was 1936. Lefty said: "Joe was as good a player as he was, and as good if not better than you."

Cobb was furious, saying: "There hasn't been a man born who could play baseball better than me." When Lefty told Cobb Joe was being groomed to replace Babe Ruth in New York, Ty was deeply impressed and said, "I had to meet this young lad."

The three of them met in the bar at the Top of the Mark, Mark Hopkins Hotel in San Francisco. Joe was immaculately attired in an elegant suit and tie. Joe was always stylish in his attire. He had a refined, gracious and dignified personality.

At the meeting with Joe, Cobb said, "Joe was quiet and well-mannered with a steely look of determination in his eyes that belied his eighteen years. He had an aura of confidence about him that reminded me of me when I was his age." Cobb later told Lefty: "I was convinced he was going to make it big in New York."

Joseph Paul (The Yankee Clipper) DiMaggio

Joe DiMaggio, nicknamed "Joltin' Joe" or "The Yankee Clipper" was one of the most popular and outstanding players in the Majors from the mid-thirties until he retired in 1951. Joe was a symbol of talent, commitment and achievement. He helped the Yankees win nine World Series championships from 1936 to 1951.

He won the Most Valuable Player award three times. It was his fifty-six game-hitting streak in 1941 that mesmerized the nation and helped him beat out Ted Williams, who hit .406 that year for MVP award.

Ty Cobb said, "DiMaggio's hitting streak is a record that will never be broken."

In 1933, DiMaggio was signed to play for the San Francisco Seals in the Pacific Coast League. During his first full season with the Seals, Joe batted .340 with 28 home runs and put together a 61-game hitting streak. After two more spectacular seasons with the Seals, in which he hit .341 and .398, his contract was sold to the New York Yankees.

The Yankees sent Joe a contract in 1936 for $5000.00. Joe wasn't happy with the offer and told Lefty O'Doul about the initial offer.

Lefty told Ty (who was a prolific letter writer, always signing his letters in his trademark green ink) that Joe was having difficulty getting the money he wanted from the Yankees. Lefty asked if Ty would help Joe get the money he wanted.

Ty offered to help Joe. Cobb was a successful financial negotiator when he was with the Tigers, and offered to write a letter for Joe to the Yankee General Manager, Ed Barrow.

When Joe received a 2nd contract for $6000.00, Ty said it still wasn't enough money, and suggested another letter for Joe to send to Mr. Barrow.

Joe received a 3rd contract for $8500 with a letter attached from Barrow saying, "This is our final offer, take it or leave it, and Joe - and tell Ty Cobb to stop writing letters for you." Joe signed, and he and Ty became lifetime friends.

DiMaggio made his debut as a Yankee on May 3, 1936. During his rookie season, he batted .323 with 29 home runs, helping the Bronx Bombers win a World Series Championship. With Joe's help, the Yankees won four consecutive (1936-39) World Series Championships, making him the only athlete in the history of North American professional sports to win championships in each of his first four seasons.

On January 14, 1954, Joe captured the heart of the beautiful, glamorous Hollywood star Marilyn Monroe. The marriage captured the headlines in papers across the country. They were married in San Francisco. The couple would break up six months later.

During his 13 seasons in Major League Baseball, DiMaggio won nine World Series Championships and three American League MVP awards. He had a career batting average of .325, with .361 career home runs. DiMaggio was inducted into the National Baseball Hall of Fame in 1955.

Ty was long retired, and out of the game and the headlines. He enjoyed giving advice to young players like Joe DiMaggio, suggesting he use a lighter bat and not take fielding practice in the outfield during the hot August days: "It would wear you out." Ty would say.

Joe was a pull hitter, and Ty would suggest he hit more to left. "Use the entire field," he would tell him. "Try bunting," Ty advised Joe. Joe smiled, listened, quietly and being a gentleman, but did not take Ty's advice.

Cobb Becomes Tigers Manager

In 1921 Cobb became the player-manager of the Tigers. The team improved under Cobb, but other than 1924 the Tigers were not a factor in the pennant race under his leadership. However, Ty was a master batting coach, and he had a great deal to do with the development of Tigers hitters, especially future Hall of Famer Harry Heilmann.[20]

"Harry Heilmann was one of the most marvelous men I ever met in baseball and one of the greatest right-handed hitters. He had a choppy but powerful stroke. He was a tough man to pitch to." Cobb said.

In 1926 the Tigers fell to sixth place in the American League. It was no surprise when on November 3, 1926, Cobb announced that he was stepping down as manager of the Tigers and retiring from baseball.

However, he signed a two-year contract to play for the Philadelphia Athletics in 1927 and 1928. At seasons end, he retired from baseball at the age of forty-two.

Quotes about Cobb: "I'm glad to pay tribute to the greatest of all ballplayers, and to my esteemed friend. More than any man in the history of baseball, Ty Cobb has combined the arts of all aspects of the game, and used them with a really brilliant mind." - Walter Johnson, 1927 (Hall of Fame, 1936)

Cobb hitting tips: "Aim to smack the ball back at the pitcher - this will result in more hits up the middle."

---

[20] Heilmann was 19 years old when he broke into the big leagues. He played for the Tigers from 1914-29. He won four batting titles, 1921-23-25-27. He hit .403 in 1923. His lifetime BAV was .342. He was elected into the Hall of Fame in 1952.

CHAPTER SEVEN
Field of Dreams

Cobb quotes: "No game is hopefully lost until the last man is out. Never hold the ball. Get it back in play as quickly as possible. Fractions of seconds count and are too valuable to waste when you are taking part in a play that may save a score."

"Tyrus Cobb is sorely in need of a good press agent, just like Babe Ruth had," said Ernie Harwell who paid tribute to Ty at Tiger Stadium after his death on July 17,1961.[21]

Field of Dreams is considered one of the all-time best baseball films ever made. The film was released in April 1989 and starred Kevin Costner as an Iowa farmer who hears a mysterious voice in his cornfield saying to him, "if you build it, they will come." Later the ghosts of great players attend and play a game. There is an amusing scene when the farmer approaches the players as they come out of the cornfield led by Shoeless Joe Jackson.[22]

---

[21] William Earnest (Ernie) Harwell was a Hall of Fame sportscaster best known for his long career calling Major League Baseball games. He spent 42 of his 55 years with the Detroit Tigers on radio and television.

[22] Joseph J. (Shoeless Joe) Jackson is best remembered for his alleged connection with seven other Chicago White Sox players who participated in a conspiracy to fix the 1919 World Series. Baseball's first commissioner, Kenesaw Mountain Landis banned them all from playing baseball for life. His lifetime batting average of .356 is third best in baseball.

Kevin asks Joe: "Where's Ty Cobb?"

Joe answers, "Cobb wanted to play, but we told him to stick it. We didn't like the SOB when he was alive, we don't want to play with him now that he's dead." That's a humorous line but not true. Ty admired Joe's playing ability, and when Joe was banned from playing baseball, Ty helped him financially.

Baseball's First Millionaire Player

As a young player for the Tigers, Cobb hung out with stockbrokers who drank at a downtown Detroit watering hole. He gave them inside baseball gossip and signed balls and photos; they gave him tips on the stock market.

Ty invested what little he earned, and monies he received from participating in three World Series. He started investing in the stock market. He invested in upcoming corporations such as: General Electric, R.J. Reynolds Tobacco, U.S. Steel and a small motor car company that gobbled up other small car manufactures and eventually became General Motors.

He made some profits from his investments and a few of his teammates called him lucky. "Suck luck, only suckers rely on luck. I studied the market and made my own luck." Ty said.

In the early twenties, Ty's good friend and hunting partner in Atlanta, Robert Woodruff told him his company bought a small soda pop company in Atlanta for twenty-five million dollars and he should invest in it.

Ty invested about $10.000 in a little-known Southern beverage company in Atlanta called Coca-Cola and eventually owned over 20,000 shares valued at over four million. (See chapter eleven)

"While golfing with President Eisenhower one day on the 5th green at Augusta, where they play the Masters, the president told Ty: "During World War II, GI's drank over five billion bottles of coke.""

He gave stock tips to his teammates and urged them to invest for the future, though few had the inclination or resources to do so.

He used his great wealth due to his shrewd investments that contributed to his early success to establish the Cobb Memorial Hospital in Royston. The hospital is now one of the crown jewels of an integrated rural healthcare system that serves thousands of families throughout northeast Georgia. Another Cobb-funded hospital opened in Livonia, Georgia on July 1, 2012.

Ty believed so strongly in Coca-Cola that he purchased three Coca-Cola bottling plants, located in Boise, Idaho, Oregon and Santa Maria, California.

Cobb was an astute businessman. His investments in cotton futures, beer distributorships, a tire distributorship in Augusta, Georgia, home building and a copper mine in Bisbee, Arizona added to his fortune. He also built the first apartment building in Augusta, Georgia.

Cobb was one of the first ballplayers to endorse products such as cigarettes, tobacco, laxatives, chewing gum and Louisville Slugger, the only bat he ever used. These endorsements added to his growing bank account.

Although Cobb's top annual salary as a baseball player was less than $40,000 (including bonuses), his shrewd investments made him such a financial success that at his death in July 1961, his net worth was about fifteen million dollars.

Cobb Testifies at the House of Representatives

Ty always enjoyed visiting Washington whether it was to play the Senators, visit a friend in the White House, or testify before a Congressional Committee in the House of Representatives, as he did in 1951.

The House was looking into the Reserve Clause. This was the ruling that bound players to their teams for life and was widely accepted by the owners and players, who had no freedom in determining their fates and destinations. He believed and told the Congressmen that ruling made slaves of the players and was a violation of anti-trust laws.

"I testified for over an hour and outlined my plan allowing players who played for their club for five years to become a free agent after the fifth year enabling players to sell their services to the highest bidder. I told the committee that was the American way." Cobb said.

Ty realized he was ahead of the times, because the House disagreed with him, but he believed in the future that baseball and the Supreme Court would come around to his way of thinking.

In 1969, center fielder Curt Flood of the St. Louis Cardinals wrote a letter to Bowie Kuhn, the Commissioner of major league baseball, protesting the Cardinals' decision to trade him to the Philadelphia Phillies and asked to be made a free agent. The Supreme Court ruled against Flood in a 5-3 decision in 1972. In December 1975, the players finally won the right to free agency, when arbitrator Peter Seitz ruled that the reserve clause granted a team only one additional year of service from a player, putting an end to perpetual renewal rights the clubs had claimed for so long.

Quotes about Cobb: "Cobb's aggressive exploits on the diamond brought high drama to the game. He seems to have understood from early in his professional career, that competition in baseball, as in war, defensive strategy never has produced ultimate victory." ~General Douglas Mac Arthur

Hitting tips: If you have trouble hitting high inside fastballs, crouch over from the waist and pass them up. Crouching makes the pitcher throw lower. That forces him away from the position that bothers you. This will allow you to hit the pitch you like.

Cobb statistical records: Cobb holds the record for batting over 300 twenty-three consecutive years.

Cobb statistical records: Cobb holds the record for most steals of home – 54.

Cobb Fact: Cobb was always willing to talk to fans, at home and on the road, freely signing autographs for fans and especially children.

Cobb Fact: He answered his fan mail always writing and signing his name with his signature green ink pen.

CHAPTER EIGHT
Ty Cobb and Babe Ruth

Cobb quotes:
"I regret to this day that I never went to college. I feel I should have been a doctor."

At the turn of the century, Baltimore was the sixth largest city in America. It has since slipped to twenty-first. It was a rough, tough city with many blue-collar, hard working men. The roughest part of the city was a section known as Pigtown, where George was born.

It was here that George Herman (Babe) Ruth was born on February 6, 1895. Six of George's siblings would die in childhood, and George's parents would also die when George was young. His mother passed away from tuberculosis, and his father, who was a bartender downstairs while the family lived above the bar, was killed in a knife fight outside the saloon.

Ruth's biography opens with the line, "I was a bad kid." Later in the book, his biographer writes, "I hardly knew my parents," Ruth says. Ruth was not a very attentive son. He states in his book that his mother died when he was thirteen, in fact he was sixteen. The saloon where George grew up is no longer there. It would now be in centerfield in Camden Yards, home of the Baltimore Orioles. Fittingly, Ruth made his professional start in baseball in Baltimore where he acquired his nickname, "Babe."

When George was seven, he could be seen running around Pigtown smoking cigarettes, cigars, drinking beer in his father's bar, shoplifting and cussing up a storm so bad that sailors would blush. His parents claimed George was irredeemable. His father placed him in an orphanage called, Saint Mary's School for wayward, delinquent and incorrigible boys. He went in at seven, and came out at nineteen.

It is alleged that George's father signed over custody of his son to the Xaverian Brothers, a Catholic Order of Jesuit Missionaries who operated St. Mary's.

Around the turn of the century, many schools around the East Coast, like St. Mary's were both an orphanage and reformatory. There were about 800 children at the orphanage. His parents never came to see George while he was there.

It was though an angel was watching over George when he met Brother Mathias. The Brother was the main disciplinarian at the school, who knew of George's lack of love and discipline at home, and took George under his wing. The Brother spent much time with George providing the guidance and support George needed. The school had many baseball teams; it was Brother Mathias who helped George develop as a baseball player.

George had grown to six feet and weighed 190 pounds at thirteen. He was amazed at how far the Brother could hit the ball. George observed Mathias' swing that was upward, a swing George developed at a young age, and parlayed that swing throughout his baseball career. When George became famous as

"The Babe" in New York, he came to develop a love for children and went out of his way to provide love, autographs, photos and time to do things for children, especially those in need.

Baseball was the prime type of recreation for the boys, and George played every position displaying potential not usually seen from boys his age. He developed as an excellent pitcher and could hit with power and evolved as a potential professional prospect.

On February 27, 1914, at nineteen, Jack Dunn, the manager of the Baltimore Orioles, a minor league franchise in the International League signed George to a contract to play for his team. George's parents had signed custody of George to the school; to avoid any legal problems, Dunn became George's legal guardian.

Jack Dunn was a well-known scout with an eye for recognizing youngsters with talent, and he saw in George a young, accomplished and potentially brilliant future star. When George showed up at the ballpark with Dunn, other players started cracking jokes about the new kid, and one of them said: "Look, there's Jack's newest Babe." Other players started calling George "Babe," and thus was born George Herman "Babe" Ruth.

George spent thirteen years at the orphanage, and had never been in a hotel until he arrived in Baltimore. A big treat at St. Mary's was to have a hotdog on Sunday. When he was told he could order anything he wanted in the hotel coffee shop, George went wild ordering several steaks, four eggs, piles of potatoes and an ice cream sundae for dessert. He had never been in an elevator and enjoyed riding the elevator up and down like a kid, which he was, mentally and emotionally. He bought a bicycle, and enjoyed riding it around town. It was at this time he discovered girls.

Five months after George signed with the Orioles, his contract was sold to the Boston Red Sox. It was extremely rare for an untried young boy of nineteen to jump from a minor league team to the Majors, but on July 11, 1914, young George made his major league debut against the Cleveland Indians, then known as the Naps. Boston won 4-3, and Ruth was credited with the win.

Ruth went on to win eighty-nine games for the Red Sox, including three in the World Series, leading Boston to two Championships. He hit 49 home runs for Boston, 649 for the Yankees and 6 for the Boston Braves at the end of his career, for a record of 714 lifetime hits.

Ty Cobb was the king of baseball until the loud, muscular, uneducated tall young man from Baltimore, Maryland arrived in Boston in 1914. Ruth would eventually knock Cobb off his mighty big throne, much to Ty's dismay. He could not have imagined that one day the fat kid on the mound would be his principal rival, change the game and battle him for glory.

Little did anyone know that when Ruth was traded from Boston to New York after the 1919 season, that he would become the bellwether in baseball, and change the game that Cobb so loved. The science or cerebral style of baseball that Ty played -- the bunt, the chop, the steal or double steal, the hit and run -- was about to change. At no time in baseball history had two men played at the same time and changed the game we know as the National Pastime.

They met on May 11, 1915 in Detroit, when the Red Sox came to town. Ruth was twenty when he faced Cobb for the first time. Ruth knew about Ty's reputation as the greatest player in baseball. The brash young man yelled at Ty when he stepped into the batter's box, "Fastball coming Ty," daring him to hit it. Cobb greeted the cocky kid with a line single to right to start the first inning.[23]

Ruth walked Cobb on his next at bat. The Tigers went on the beat Boston, 5-1. This would be the first of many battles to come between the two titans of baseball, both on and off the field. Cobb faced Ruth 67 times and had 22 hits for a .328 BAV. Facing the young rookie, Cobb was the highest paid player in the game. He was the smartest, fastest, most competitive, the biggest drawing card, a terror on the base paths and an inspiration to young boys across the country. Ruth had heard all about the Peach.

Ty looked at the youngster, standing 60 feet 6 inches from him, carrying his three bats on his shoulder to terrify the pitcher, as he always did. Looking at the smooth-faced youngster from Baltimore, Ty was thinking: "Here is another young kid up for a look-see, and bound to fail." Ty thought George was too heavy, too slow and could not throw as fast as

Walter Johnson. Ty believed George was doomed to failure, like so many others before him.

The two men were as different as day and night. Cobb was a Baptist, born in the Deep South. Ruth, a Catholic, was born in the North. Cobb was raised in a middle class family; Ruth was raised in a poverty-stricken home. Cobb was raised by a loving mother and an intelligent father. Ruth was raised by his father, a bartender working in a saloon. Ty had a pleasant youth, raised in rural Royston, Georgia, working on his father's farm; Ruth was raised in an orphanage. Ruth was abandoned his parents.

The collision between the young Babe Ruth, age 19 when he arrived in Boston in 1914 and the aging, superstar of the Deadball Era would create media and fan frenzy for the next fourteen years. Ty was twenty-nine at the time. Thus began a struggle for baseball dominance between two of the most competitive men playing the game at that time.

The two great stars took different paths to their fame and fortune. Cobb played small ball, using the scientific approach to the game. Hit the ball where they ain't, steal bases, speed and daring, rattling his opponents. Ruth, with his heavy 48-ounce bat and upward swing, hit the ball over the fence.

Ruth introduced fans to the home run, fans loved it then, and they still do. Players and fans in the Deadball Era thought the home run was a trick play, and looked down on it. Ty was approaching the end of his career. He was older, wiser and began to admire the happy home run hitter, and eventually, Ruth appreciated the game Ty played.

Ruth spent six seasons with the Boston Red Sox, 1914-1919 as a pitcher. He became one of the preeminent southpaws in baseball helping Boston achieve two World Series titles while winning three games in the Series.

Babe Ruth, Red Sox, 1914

The Babe blossomed as a pitcher in 1916 winning 23 while losing 13. This helped the Red Sox defeat Brooklyn 4-1 in the World Series. Ruth allowed the Dodgers only five hits in game 2 won by the Red Sox 2-1 in a game that went 14 innings. Ruth pitched 13 innings of shutout ball.

In 1918, Ruth pitched game one beating the Chicago Cubs 1-0 giving him 22 consecutive innings of shutout ball. He pitched game four defeating the Cubs 3-2. This set a World Series record by pitching 29-2/3 innings of scoreless ball. That record stood until 1961 when the great Whitey Ford of the New York Yankees broke Ruth's record.

Ruth's fame, after arriving in New York in 1920 created a national frenzy of fan support, the desire to see his photo in the newspapers or sports magazine created an industry of sports writers, vying for his attention.

The Babe's fame had even exceeded the president. One time on a train trip through the Midwest, the train stopped in a little town in Illinois, a whistle stop. It was about ten o'clock in the evening, he train halted to obtain water for its engine. It was pouring down buckets of rain, and no one expected anyone to be at the station at that time, except the men working at the station.

The train stopped for only ten minutes to get water, but when the reporters and players on board peered out the windows, they were amazed to see a crowd of over four thousand people just waiting to see the Babe, reported by a New York Times sports writer.

New balls were not put into play in the Deadball Era as in today's game. Pitchers spit on the ball, cut the ball with a nail or emery board, or on their belt buckle causing the ball to fly in a weird path to the plate. These tactics made hitting home runs difficult. The Majors banned these schemes in the early twenties.

Ruth played some outfield for Boston in 1918 hitting 11 home runs. In 1919, he won 9 and lost 5 but broke the Major League record for home runs with 29. He hit 49 home runs during his career in Boston.

After the 1919 season, Ruth was sold to the New York Yankees by Sox owner Harry Frazee, a theatrical agent, producer and director of Broadway shows. He had financial problems forcing him to trade Ruth to Yankees for $125.000, an unheard of amount of money in those days. Ruth won 89, lost 46, had 17 shutouts and hit 49 home runs while in Boston. It would be 86 years or until 2004 when the Red Sox beat St. Louis to end the "Curse of the Bambino."

Although Ruth was a great pitcher and hitting home runs to the amazement and fascination of the fans, he was constantly in trouble with management. His boozing, gambling, huge money demands and troublesome ways caused the Boston owner and theater producer, who was in financial debt to sell Ruth to the Yankees, causing the "Curse of the Bambino" to come into existence.

In 1920, Ruth hit 54 homers in his first year with the Yankees. He blasted an unheard of 59 in 1921 and 60 in 1927. The Yankees built Yankee Stadium and opened it in 1923. The press called it the House the Ruth built.

Babe Ruth and Cobb were bitter enemies during their playing days, they became good friends after they retired. They fished, hunted and enjoyed playing golf.

Ruth changed the game Cobb so loved and played so well. Baseball would never be the same. The New York media saw in Ruth not just a new champion, but also a man who would eventually come to symbolize a changing America. He loved women, fancy cars, winning, eating big, drinking big, hitting big, and having fun. George was not a good driver; if he wrecked a car, he simply bought another.

He loved wearing a fur coat, and he didn't care what anyone thought. When asked what his approach to the game was, Ruth said, "I swing big, with everything I've got. I hit big or I miss big. I like to live as big as I can."

America was changing in many ways. The economy was booming and wages had increased for many people. Wall Street made it easy for people to buy stock with a small down payment, and many did. Eventually, this would cause the market to crash in late October 1929, causing the greatest depression the nation had ever seen.

Young soldiers returning from the war wanted to try new ways of living. Baseball had never been so popular. Woman received the right to vote when the 19th Amendment to the U.S. Constitution was ratified on August 18, 1920.

The culture was rapidly changing. Women were smoking, drinking whiskey with men in public and having sex with men other than their husbands and listening to a new kind of music - jazz. Buildings in New York were getting taller; the stock market was raging with huge profits to me made. Baseball was being broadcast on the radio. This new era was called the "Roaring Twenties."

The Eighteenth Amendment to the Constitution was ratified by the U.S. Congress and enacted in January 1920 and remained in place until 1933. This was a nationwide constitutional ban on the production, importation, transportation, and sale of alcoholic beverages. This would eventually cause mass disobedience by the public that caught many members of the Congress and the church by surprise. It also created massive corruption and lawlessness by crime lords led by Al Capone.

Following the war, the dry crusade was revived by the national Prohibition Party, founded in 1869, and the Woman's Christian Temperance Union (WCTU), founded in 1873. The WCTU advocated the prohibition of alcohol as a method for preventing, through education, abuse from alcoholic husbands.

Cobb, with his Southern Baptist upbringing and conservative way of thinking, saw in Ruth the symbol of the corruption and the change in the culture of America that he did not approve of. Many of the changes in the culture took place in the big cities, but millions of Americans lived on farms, in small towns or rural areas and continued to live simple, quiet lives. Life was still hard for many people including blacks, foreigners, and other minority groups.

"My way of playing the game was becoming old-fashioned. Ruth changed the game, and it would never be the same. I saw Ruth as a threat to baseball, how the game should be played, and how players should behave." Ty lamented.

Cobb did not approve of Ruth's boozing, womanizing and gambling at the racetrack or casinos in Havana, Cuba. Cobb's moralizing and Southern gentleman's way of living was in direct opposition to Ruth's big city lifestyle.

Cobb was dismayed at Ruth's approach to life saying, "The Babe drank heavily and womanized his way from city to city, eating like a pig, drinking, gambling and staying up all night. I could not hide my dislike for this man who violated the rules of morality, the rules of life and the game."

Ty also said, "Ruth was worshipped by millions of fans, children loved him and the New York media wrote lovingly about him, never writing about his wayward ways, but, by golly, he could sure hit lots of home runs." Cobb admitted.

Ty continued, "We paid no attention to the frenzy caused by the media and fans. The fans argued over who was better. We paid no attention to that media circus. We went about our business playing baseball and having fun.

"Who was better?" a reporter asked Cobb. Ty replied, "What's better, vanilla or chocolate, it's your choice." In polls taken in the late twenties and early thirties, when asked who was a better player, Cobb was chosen. In the balloting for the Hall of Fame in Cooperstown, NY, Cobb finished first, Ruth second. Ruth stole 123 bases over his career. When asked how Ruth was as a runner, Cobb laughed and said, "He ran pretty good for a fat fella."

The press asked Cobb the difference between the two stars. Cobb replied, "Aside from the home runs, I believed in keeping myself in good condition, eating well and getting lots of sleep. I didn't smoke or drink alcohol. In the off-season, I exercised and ran fifteen to twenty miles every day. I always reported to spring training in good shape, not overweight and out of condition as Ruth did."

"My harassment of Ruth was continuous and sometimes vicious. I called him various names often calling him a baboon due to his lack of education. This was part of my psychological warfare with Ruth. I would get him so angry at me, he would lose his focus," Ty said.

Some people thought Ruth had black blood in him, therefore he was part Negro. Those rumors were not true. Cobb, with his Southern racist beliefs often accused Ruth of being a baboon knowing how much this would make George angry.

Ty used this as part of his strategy to throw off Ruth's focus causing many arguments between the two stars. As many a fight

Cobb had off the field, Ruth had on the field with other players and a few umpires.

"We loathed each other, not because of our competitiveness or rivalry. Because of our personalities, our way of looking at life was poles apart," Cobb declared. "We are as different as the sun and the moon," Ty said.

When a reporter asked Cobb if he hated Ruth, Cobb answered saying, "I didn't hate him, I despised him but, secretly, inwardly, I admired him greatly. He changed the game from scratch for a run or two, to hit the ball over the fence. When we came to New York to play the Yankees, the stadium was always sold out. It was always a lot of fun playing against Ruth."

Ruth wanted nothing more than to manage or coach the Yankees after he retired. The Yankees wanted no part of Ruth. Ed Barrow, Yankees
General Manager refused to give George the job exclaiming: "Ruth was unable to manage himself; how could he manage the Yankees?" Cobb believed the Babe was jealous, because he had been the manager of the Tigers from 1921 – 1926.

However, Cobb and Ruth became good friends after Ruth retired. They enjoyed each other's company, reminiscing about the good old days. They fished, hunted and played golf. Both men were excellent golfers (more about their golf in the next chapter).

Ruth passed away due to cancer in mid-August 1948. Cobb was part of half a million people who turned out to pay final respects for the Sultan of Swat in New York City. The country had a moment of silence and President Harry S. Truman said a few kind words about the Bambino.

Many years later while visiting New York, Ty drove by Ruth's elegant apartment in the upper-East Side, and said, "Lord, I sure miss that man."

Ruth ushered in a new era of long-distance hitting and high scoring, effectively bringing down the curtain on the Deadball Era. Cobb's way of playing the game was over. New and younger players coming into the game were also hitting home runs: Jimmie Foxx, Hank Greenberg, Lou Gehrig, Hack Wilson, Joe DiMaggio, Johnny Mize and Ted Williams, to name just a few.

Cobb batting tips: Don't pull a curve ball from a right-hander. The ball is revolving away from you. Hit with the revolution and to right field.

Cobb on stealing bases: "A difficult part of the game is learning the art of stealing bases. A player who can steal second in a tight game is invaluable to his team."

Cobb statistical records: He won nine consecutive batting titles between 1907- 1915 – Major League record

CHAPTER NINE
Ty the Golfer

Cobb quotes:
"I had to fight all my life to survive. They were all against me, but I beat the bastards and left them in the ditch."

In his retirement years, Ty made a few attempts to buy a major-league team. He was part of a team of investors that tried to buy the Cincinnati Reds in 1929 and later the Detroit Tigers in the early thirties. Both attempts failed.

In his post-baseball career, The Georgia Peach took up golf. Cobb, unlike a majority of his contemporaries, made a fortune away from baseball. He had invested in both Coca-Cola and General Motors in the early days of the soft drink and auto industries.

Cobb turned some portion of that money to investing in his golf game. He hired the most reputable teachers of the day including the great Bobby Jones. He became a member at several country clubs across the country including Olympic Club in San Francisco and the Augusta National where played the Masters.

He enjoyed attending old-timers games, visiting Cooperstown swapping tales of the good old days, talking with his contemporaries, and playing golf. He used the most

NORM COLEMAN

expensive clubs to play with Bobby Jones, Ben Hogan, Sam Snead and President Dwight D. Eisenhower.

Given Cobb's personality and viral nature, a famed sportswriter wrote of Ty's golf game, "If ever a sport had been created for which he was wholly unsuited, it was golf."

Cobb was an avid golfer

Cobb's temperament rendered the game all but impossible. He lashed out constantly, threw tantrums all over the course. In his later days as a member of Augusta National he would barge through groups of players including Dwight D. Eisenhower.

"Once, on a golf course," Ike said, "I was about to putt on the fifth green when I heard a voice yelling, 'Get out of the way, I'm coming through.' Then the demand came again. So I made my way and Ty Cobb played right through me, without apology. I guess nobody but the great Cobb would dare do that to a president." The secret service was concerned about the interruption and drew their pistols but the President told them,

"It's OK, it's only Ty Cobb coming through."

Cobb wasn't particularly good at golf. In his best days he shot in the mid 80's, low 90's range. He was beaten quite often in match play. Babe Didrikson, a pioneer of the women's game, took Cobb down 8 and 7 one match. At Olympic in 1939, he faced a 12 year old in the club championship. The boy beat Cobb easily. The latter never returned to the club.

One moment of triumph overshadowed all of Cobb's frustrations in golf. For years, the bitter Georgian bemoaned Babe Ruth's effect on baseball. Hitting was an art, a science. Ruth had turned it into a mindless activity. Yet the fans adored Ruth more for his slugging than they ever did Cobb for his ability to find gaps in an opponent's defense. Cobb resented Ruth for that reason, but never really got the chance to challenge the Yankee outfielder because he was well into his thirties when Ruth left the pitcher's mound for good.

When the opportunity arrived for Cobb to take on the Babe in a major golf tournament, he took advantage of the situation. He would face the golf course in front of a large gathering of the press and the public.

In a much-celebrated match in 1941, the two giants of the game of baseball engaged in a 54-hole affair. Ruth was the favorite. He carried a six-to-eight handicap according to Stump, nearly half of Cobb's on his best day.

"There have been several great matches in golf history, but few can compare to Ruth vs. Cobb in the Has-Been's Golf Championship." a golf writer said.

Cobb Quotes: "The crowd makes the game. I love playing in a park with a sold out crowd, especially on the road. I work harder when the fans are against me. A large crowd booing me gets my energy up. The two worst parks for fans 'riding' me are St. Louis and Philadelphia."

Quotes about Cobb: "I saw Cobb play a game with a temperature of 103 with a leg wrapped in bandages. Doctors ordered him not to play. He got three hits, stole three bases and won the game." - Grantland Rice

CHAPTER TEN
Cobb vs. Ruth: "The Has-Been's Championship"

Cobb quotes:
"When I played, I didn't play for fun. I played to win. Second place didn't interest me. Baseball is a red-blooded sport for red-blooded men. It's no pink tea, and mollycoddles had better stay out. It's a contest and everything that implies, a struggle for supremacy, a survival of the fittest."

The two superstars and future Hall of Famers had fought their battles for fourteen years at Navin Field in Detroit and Yankee Stadium in New York.

Cobb was the undisputed king of baseball in the early days of the new Century. Ty was defending his batting title in 1915 having won eight titles in a row since 1907. He would make the current season his ninth consecutive year as batting champ, a record he still holds.

They first met at Navin Field on May 11th 1915. Ty hit a single the first time he faced Ruth. Ty was 2 for 2 with a walk against Ruth in a game won by the Tigers 5-1.[24] Ruth showed no fear as he faced the great Cobb for the first time.

---

[24] Tom Stanton, *Ty and The Babe: Baseball's Fiercest Rivals: A Surprising Friendship and the 1941 Has-Beens Golf Championship* (New York: St. Martin's Press, 2008)

Babe Ruth and Ty played many golf tournaments after the Babe retired. In early 1941, the two retired Hall of Famers were approached by a high ranking general in the Pentagon who asked both men them if they would play a best two of three golf tournament to raise money for war bonds. They accepted, and earned millions for the military.

The tournament between the two titans of baseball created national headlines and brought both giants of baseball into the spotlight once again.

They became good friends after Ruth retired. Ty loved the golf game for relaxation and competitiveness. Ruth could hold his own on the golf course. Cobb eagerly accepted believing he could easily beat the Babe proving once and for all time, he was the better athlete. George had no doubt he could crush Ty.

They agreed to play in this ballyhooed 54-hole tournament covered by mass media. Cobb brought in Walter Hagen to be his personal coach.[25] They agreed all monies raised would be provided to buy war bonds for the military.

The Peach was embarrassed when he lost a match to Babe Didrikson, a pioneer of the women's game. She was a woman way ahead of her time. A second embarrassing loss was to a twelve-year-old boy in the club championship in 1939 at the Olympic Club in San Francisco. Ty never returned to the club after this loss.

The 54-hole tournament covered by mass media brought the two men back into the public eye for the first time since Cobb & Ruth retired.

---

[25] Walter Charles Hagen was an American professional golfer and a major figure in golf in the first half of the 20th century. His tally of 11 professional majors is third behind Jack Nicklaus and Tiger Woods.

First Match: Newton Commonwealth Golf Course, Newton, Mass.

The Newton Commonwealth Golf Course is an 18-hole public golf course located in Newton, Massachusetts, just outside the city of Boston. This course was originally created as a nine-hole course in 1897 and was previously named the Commonwealth Club.

Ruth had a warm heart for wayward, troubled boys as he spent twelve years in an orphanage in Baltimore, Maryland. They agreed to give a portion of the monies raised to local charities for wayward boys. A motion picture starring Spencer Tracy and Mickey Rooney, *Boys Town,* had been released a few years prior to the tournament raising the public's attention to the subject.

Over a thousand spectators showed up for the first round, including former Ambassador Joseph P. Kennedy, a fan of the Babe and father of future president John F. Kennedy.

Both Ty and George were slightly nervous at the start of the match due to the large crowd although both had played baseball before large crowds. Neither had ever played golf with the amount of fans in attendance.

Cobb had difficulties on the first three rounds and Ruth poked jokingly at Ty. Cobb ignored him, never speaking to him at all during play. Ruth kidded Ty saying, "What's wrong Ty, sun too bright for you?" Ty ignored him.

Ty's game improved over the next four holes, Ruth was off his game, and complained that Ty was moving too slow. "Speed it up, move along Ty," Ruth groaned. Ty ignored him. It was a tactic Ty used to get George upset and off his game when they played baseball.

Over the last four holes, Cobb held a slight lead, and at the end of the eighteenth, the score was Cobb 81 Ruth 83.

Cobb beamed as he headed to the clubhouse. Ruth shook his hand telling him, "Nice game Ty." Cobb told reporters standing near the two men, "I finally beat the Babe at something." Everyone laughed as flash bulbs flashed. The two men posed with several young boys, George's hand on the boys shoulder, all smiling broadly for the press. The fans were delighted and clapped as they entered the clubhouse.

The media and fans had argued for years about who was the better athlete. Cobb maintained that he was, because he finished first in the balloting for the Hall of Fame in 1936. Ty always believe he was the best because of his hitting, running and lifetime BAV of .367 to Ruth's .342.

Ruth and his adoring fans and New York media believed Ruth was because of his home run production, 714, and his great pitching prowess for the Red Sox, leading the Red Sox and Yankees to six World Series titles. Ruth reminded Ty he had won none. But Ty reminded George he was first into the Hall of Fame, "And you finished second George." Both men laughed and George said, "I'll drink to that."

As to who was the better athlete, Ty believed the winner of the tournament would answer the question and he believed it would be him. At the end of the first round, Ruth was heard commentating to a reporter that, "Cobb was the better player."

Second Match: Fresh Meadow Country Club, Flushing, NY

Fresh Meadow Country Club is a golf course in the Eastern United States, located on Long Island in Lake Success, New York, its home since 1946.

In the beginning, Fresh Meadow traveled first class. The members wanted their course to be one of the country's great examples of golf, up to testing the leading players in major competition.

The course was considered one of the best in the country by *American Golfer* magazine. Ruth had played this course many times, and had always played well. He felt extremely confident going in.

Ruth's conviction in his ability to win this match enabled him to tell reporters how he felt, and he boasted, "I will beat Cobb today." Some reporters told Ty what Ruth said. Cobb laughed saying, "Ruth is under pressure to win, and he will wilt. Having won the first match is like winning the first game of the World Series." "I am not concerned," Ty replied.

Newspapers in New York and Detroit were publishing stories of the tournament, as were papers across the country. Both men were delighted to be back in the news again.

Ruth complained again that Ty was too slow, sleep-walking across the greens. Cobb laughed saying, "I play slow and deliberately." He also knew this style of play would disturb Ruth, upsetting his focus.

The two men fought the difficult course over the first four holes, with Ruth leading Ty by 2. Knowing Cobb's penchant for losing his temper on the diamond, fans and reporters were waiting for Ty to lose it today, golf being a frustrating sport. He restrained his temper, much to the surprise of the press and Ruth.

The next four holes were difficult for the Babe, whose game was off due to the difficult course. Cobb did not have the same problems George was having, his playing improved. By the end of eight holes, Ty moved ahead by 2 strokes. By the end of the seventeenth hole, the two men were tied.

They played the difficult eighteenth hole and both shot a par 4 forcing a play-off.

On the nineteenth hole, Ruth was on the green in two strokes, Ty took three strokes to reach the green. Both men took one stroke to get close to the hole. Ruth sank his second stroke. Cobb blew a six-foot putt and finished one stroke behind the Babe. The crowd, clearly rooting for Ruth cheered as Cobb looked disconsolate. Ruth won, accepting the cheers and congratulations from his fans, forcing a final match in Michigan.

Cobb was fuming in the locker room after the match. He hated losing; second place didn't interest him. The two old friends got together in the clubhouse, the reporters hanging on their every word. Ty began to relax as Babe and Ty started talking baseball, something they enjoyed doing as much as playing golf.

A reporter asked Ruth how he pitched to Ty. Ruth said, "Easy, fast ball-high, curve low and away, fastball high, curve low, and away. If Ty or any batter dug in, I'd throw a fastball at his head. If he didn't duck, it was his bad luck. Ty never hit me like he did other pitchers."

Cobb laughed and reminded the Babe how well he did hit off him. Like many players, Ty knew his statistics. He told Ruth, "I got 22 hits off you in 67 at bats for a .328 BAV."

Ruth laughed and said, "That's true but way below your lifetime of .367." The reporters laughed as they polished off their drinks, writing down every word the two stars spoke and reminding both men they had one more match to play as they headed out of the locker room, looking forward to the next match.

Final score: Ruth 90, Cobb 91.

Third Match: Grosse Ile, Michigan.

When the first nine holes of the new course were opened in 1920, the new Grosse Ile Golf Course merged with the established Grosse Ile Country Club to form the Grosse Ile Golf and Country Club that still exists today.

Some of the wealthiest Detroit car manufacturers bought property, built mansions, joined the country club and played golf at the Grosse Ile.

The war was raging in Europe in the summer of 1941. Germany had invaded Russia while America stayed out of the war though helping Britain with its lend-lease program. The public and press were demanding ballplayers join the military

Hank Greenberg, home run slugger for the Detroit Tigers was one of the first stars to join the military. Cobb, a Captain in World War 1 congratulated the Jewish star.

Other players like Bob Feller, Ted Williams, Joe DiMaggio and golfers-like Sammy Snead, Bobby Jones and Ben Hogan also joined the military.

Walter Hagan was a great golfer and Ty's friend, coach and a huge baseball fan. He golfed frequently with Ruth and said he was a fine golfer. He advised Cobb before the matches started of Ruth's golf weakness. He tended to tire and get sloppy after the 11th or 12th hole and was bothered by slow playing golfers.

Ty took advantage of Ruth's tendency, which is why he played extra slowly during the first two matches. He planned to slow down his game and played cautiously for the final match. Cobb, as he did in baseball, studied every detail of the course, speaking to other golfers who played Grosse Ile but more importantly, he hired a young fifteen year old who Hagan told him of. The young man was Pete Devaney, whose father was an exceptional golfer and a regular on the course. Pete lived on the course and knew it like the back of his hand. Pete had never caddied for anyone but his dad and looked forward to caddying for Ty.

Just as Ty used his notebook to record every detail on pitchers, catchers and hitters when he played, he recorded the suggestions Pete provided him.

It was a hot, humid sunny day on July 20, 1941 with over 3000 people roaming around the country club when Ty and the Babe prepared to start the final match at four o'clock. When asked, the reporters sensed this was a Ty Cobb crowd.

Ruth and Cobb posing for the press

Cobb also felt that the older Michigan crowd were many of his fans, who probably saw him play in Detroit when he was the king of baseball. He was anxious like he never was when he played for the Tigers. He believed they were there to watch him beat the Babe, and he did not want to disappoint them.

Reporters asked several fans why they were there. Many said, "I want to see if Cobb still has the intense competitiveness he had when I saw him play many years ago."

Ruth was relaxed as he wandered around the clubhouse prior to the start, laughing, telling jokes to friends and reporters, being the bumptious man he was when he played with the Yankees when he was younger.

A reporter asked George how he felt. Ruth said, "Loose and relaxed."

Ruth proposed a bet on the outcome saying to Ty, "I got a thousand bucks I beat you." Ty shrugged him off; Ty did not like to gamble.

It was broiling hot as they teed off at the first hole. Both men were sweating profusely. They were tied at the end of four holes, but Ruth was not playing his game in the next four holes and fell behind Ty at the end of the eighth hole.

At the end of the thirteenth hole, Ty was up by three. Ruth seemed to realize he was doomed as he joshed with fans, lying down on the grass, having a good time, playing the good old boy, with not a care in the world as he faced defeat. The fans appeared to rally around the Babe, urging him play harder, not to give up. George winked at a few women who cheered him on as Cobb continued to play his game, conferring with his caddy on a few shots, playing slowly, carefully realizing he was wearing George down. He smelled victory but he knew it was never over until it's over.

George rallied over the next two holes, closing the gap to two behind Ty. On the fourteenth hole, Ty, facing a forty-foot putt, glanced over at Ruth. George shook his head as if to say, no way you make it. Ty, kneeled down, measuring the shot, spoke to his caddy, and approached the shot with confidence. He sank the putt, thrilling his fans as Ruth shook his head as if he could not believe what his eyes saw.

Play lasted four hours as the sun was slowly dropping in the darkening sky, and they approached the seventeenth hole. George missed a ten-foot putt while Ty easily putted a six-footer moving three strokes ahead as they neared the final hole. The match was basically over, Ty relaxed and gave his adoring fans a big smile as they cheered loudly and long, realizing Cobb would win.

Play ended as Cobb was declared the winner. Ruth approached Ty, shaking hands as Ruth congratulated Ty. The Peach was gracious, telling George he played a great game.

At the end of the match, Cobb told several reporters who gathered around him, "Winning the tournament proved once and for all time, I was the better athlete." Ty was so proud of winning the tournament he placed the "Ruth Cup" on his mantle next to his Baseball Hall of Fame plaque."

Final score: Cobb 78, Ruth 81

Theodore (Ted) Williams

Although Cobb admired Theodore (Teddy Ballgame or the Splendid Splinter) Williams, he claimed Ted could have been a better hitter if only he had listened to Ty's batting tips. Williams was notorious for listening to no one except himself.

"Ted was a natural hitter but was an obstinate fella, he pulled the ball too much instead of slapping the ball to left, losing many hits," Ty said.

"When they pulled the shift on him, placing three fielders on the right side of the infield, I suggested Ted on occasion drop a bunt down the line to third, or punch the ball through the opening on the left side of the field, but Teddy was too stubborn," the Peach claimed.

In the 1946 World Series, the St. Louis Cardinals successfully pulled a shift on Ted holding him to 5 hits in 25 AB's or a .200 BAV.

It is extremely difficult to give batting advice to anyone who hits over .400 as Williams did in 1941 hitting .406. Ted was the last player to hit over .400.

"I reminded Ted that I hit over .400 three times and he could have hit over .400 at least four times if he took my advice, but he was stubborn as a mule," Ty said, shaking his head. Williams, one of the greatest hitters in the modern era, never took batting instruction from anyone.

Williams hit 521 home runs over an eighteen-year career or an average of 29 homers per year. He lost 4 years to military service in WWII and 1½ years during the Korean War, where he served as a jet fighter pilot. He flew next to future Astronaut John Glenn who later became the first man to fly into outer space. Had he not lost those years, he could possibly have hit an additional 130 homers for a lifetime total of 650.

Near the end of Ty's life, suffering from cancer, he travelled to Scottsdale, Arizona in March 1959 where the Red Sox were engaged in spring training. Cobb was extremely tired and didn't socialize much, but entertained baseball luminaries in his motel room.

One hot spring afternoon, while resting in his room, he heard a knock on his door. "Who the hell is it?" Ty yelled. A voice from outside boomed, "Ted."

"Ted who?" responded Ty. "Ted Williams you damn old fool, open the damn door," boomed Ted in that loud voice he was known for.

Cobb invited Ted into his room along with Ted's driver. Cobb immediately poured three tall glasses of vodka and orange juice, and the two old friends, two of the greatest hitters baseball had ever seen sipped their drinks and started talking baseball as they had done so many times in the past.

Ty grumbled about how the modern players couldn't hold the jock straps of the boys who played when he did. Like many an old timer, he said the game was better when he played and the players were better too. Ted vehemently disagreed.

Cobb moaned about how the current bunch of boys struck out too much because all they wanted to do was hit home runs.

Williams more than held his own, referring to players like him; Joe DiMaggio, Stan Musial, Jackie Robinson, Hank Greenberg and Jimmy Fox. When he mentioned Babe Ruth, Ty, who never liked the Babe, pounded his fist on the table and said, "He ran pretty good for a fat fella." Both men laughed their heads off as this is territory they had covered many times in the past.

They argued over other subjects like what was the best restaurant in New York, or the finest car, the most beautiful woman, the best pitcher they ever saw or even the best soap to use when cleaning baseball uniforms.

But when the subject came to fishing, Ted was a master. He could talk fishing for hours. Cobb listened, knowing Ted was in fishing heaven. He was as expert on this topic as he was on baseball. Ted was known to believe he was an expert on any subject.

Cobb was equally adept at handling a fishing pole, a rifle and was a good golfer.

After an hour of baseball talk, Cobb, said he was tired and needed a nap. The two old friends shook hands, hugged each other and said farewell.

Ted never saw Cobb again as he died two years later on July 17, 1961 in Atlanta.

Ted Williams Museum

The first Ted Williams Museum and Hitters Hall of Fame opened in Hernando, Florida in 1994 but due to poor attendance it closed and reopened at Tropicana Field, home of the Tampa Bay Marlins in St. Petersburg, Florida.

The Museum has attracted sports legends to its many events and featured a collection that chronicled Williams's life, including his exploits as a fighter pilot, Boston Red Sox player and accomplished fisherman.

Some of the greatest sluggers in baseball have been inducted into The Ted Williams Hall of Fame Museum. Ty Cobb and Willie Mays were in the first class in 1995. Over thirty players have been inducted.[26]

In my conversation with Dave McCarthy, General Manager of the Museum, he told me he is a good friend of Denny (The last 30 game winner) McLain.[27] Dave informed me he saw my website and "Was deeply impressed." He invited me to the festivities at the Museum, as he knew that Denny and I are friends, and he is scheduled to attend the induction of Pete Rose.

He told me he would be happy to have me attend, as Ty Cobb was the first player inducted into the Museum, and his statue is outside the Museum.

I was fortunate to attend the induction ceremony in February 2017, featuring the induction of Pete Rose and Willie Horton. Over thirty famous current ball players attended as well as hundreds of fans. This annual event and dinner takes place on the field at Tropicana Field. Fans are allowed to mingle with the

---

[26] Over thirty sluggers have been inducted. For a complete list, go to: tedwilliams.com

[27] Denny McLain pitched for the Detroit Tigers from 1963 to 1970. On September 14, 1968, in front of 33,688 fans on a Saturday in Detroit, Dennis McLain stuck out 10 batters in a 5–4 win over the Oakland Athletics to become the first 30-game winner since Jay "Dizzy" Dean (St. Louis Cardinals) in 1934. He is also the last pitcher in Major League Baseball to win 30 games in one season.

players after dinner, collect autographs and take picture with the players.

I invited my nephew, Brian Coleman, a huge baseball fan, to join me as I was a guest of Mr. McCarthy. Unfortunately, McLain was not able to make it as he was too ill to travel.

Quotes about Cobb: "He threw me more curves in money negotiations than a whole tribe of Arabs. He'd hold out until hell froze over or until he got what he demanded. Frank Navin, President Detroit Tigers 1926.

Cobb on stealing bases: "The player who can steal second when the game is on the line, and put himself in a position to score, is invaluable to his team."

Cobb statistical records: Most times stealing second base, third base and home in succession - 5 times

CHAPTER ELEVEN
Ty Cobb and Coca-Cola

Cobb quotes:
"The first advice for any youngster who would make a success of playing baseball is confidence in your own ability. Believe you can hit any pitcher, catch any fly ball and steal any base. Be confident you can do anything better than anyone else, have determination to succeed and the perseverance to work at it."

1886 turned out to be an historic year in Georgia. On May 8, one of the most popular soda pop companies in American Culture came into existence and on December 18, one of the greatest players that ever played baseball was born.

As a result, Coca-Cola became one of the most famous and profitable corporations in history, and Tyrus Raymond Cobb became an outstanding ballplayer and the first player to enter the Hall of Fame.

The destiny of these two giants became entwined not only in their birth, but because Cobb made his major debut with the Detroit Tigers on August 30, 1905 and by this time, Coca-Cola had become the most popular drink in the South.

By late 1907, Cobb was on his way to winning his first batting title, leading the Tigers to their first World Series appearance, and Coca-Cola began an advertising blitz featuring Cobb who would be on his way to winning nine consecutive batting titles.

Cobb was shown in an ad at the plate saying, "Coca-Cola will put you back in the game, relieve your thirst and cool you off."

Future ads featuring Ty endorsing the product would have him saying, "I drink Coca-Cola regularly throughout all the seasons of the year." Another had him say, "When we play a double header, I always find a drink of Coca-Cola between games that refreshes me so I can play the second game as though I had not been exercising at all."

Ty made many more commercials for Coca-Cola, but he also invested his money in the Corporation. It was his friend, Robert Woodruff of Atlanta, the son of the president of Coca-Cola who suggested to Ty in 1918 he buy stock in the company. Cobb borrowed money from Mr. Woodruff against future baseball earnings and purchased 1000 shares of Coke. He continued purchasing Coke stock for the rest of his life.

Cobb's investment in Coca-Cola made him one of the first athletes to become independently well off. He amassed a prodigious fortune over his career, and post baseball career. Ty encouraged his teammates to buy, "The Pause that Refreshes" stock. Most did not earn enough money to do so, or squandered their money on gambling, liquor and women, and often went broke.

After Ty retired, he purchased three Coca-Cola bottling plants in Santa Maria, California, Twin Falls, Idaho and Bend,

Oregon. Later, his son Herschel would manage the plant in Santa Maria.

Ty would eventually own over 20,000 shares of stock making him a major stockholder in Coke and placing him on the Board of Directors. Coke grew worldwide, making Ty's stock at his death on July 17, 1961 valued at between $10 and $12 million.

Because of his investments in Coke stock, it allowed him to establish an Educational Foundation paying college tuition for thousands of Georgia students, fund the Cobb Memorial Hospital in Royston, Georgia and the Cobb Health System for poor Georgia families.

The company released a series of cardboard posters called "All Time Winners" in 1947 introducing Ty to a new generation of baseball fans and soda pop drinkers.

In 1986, to celebrate the 100th anniversary of the birth of Coca-Cola and Ty's birth, the company produced a limited edition commemorative bottle of Coke featuring Cobb on the side. One of these bottles resides in the Hall of Fame in Cooperstown, NY.[28]

One day while golfing with President Dwight D. Eisenhower, the president told Ty, "During World War two, G.I.'s drank over five billion bottles of Coke."

Denton True (Cy) Young

Cy Young entered the Hall of Fame in 1937 one year after Cobb, Ruth, Mathewson, Johnson and Honus Wagner who were in the original class in 1936.

His record of 511 wins over a twenty-two year career is a record that will never be broken. He lost 316 games.

The Cy Young Award is given annually to the best pitchers in Major League Baseball, one each for the American League and National League. The first Cy Young award went to Don Newcombe in 1956 of the Brooklyn Dodgers with a 27-7 record. Roger Clemons holds the record winning seven times.

Young was approaching the end of his long career and was disturbed by Cobb's over the top aggressiveness. He said, "Cobb was going at the game too hard." Cy also admitted, "In my twenty-two years of playing baseball, I never saw a player with all the abilities Ty Cobb had."

Cobb faced Young toward the end of Cy's career, when he pitched for Boston, then Cleveland. By that time, Young was approaching forty and overweight, but he still threw a curveball overhand with a sharp break, sometimes sidearm and an

---

[28] Dan Holmes, baseball historian formerly at the Hall of Fame Museum.

occasional submarine-style. Cobb had 97 AB's, 33 hits and batted .340 against Cy.

Cobb studied every pitcher's movement with intensity as though his life depended on it. He noted their habits, hands and feet movements. He observed if their pick-off attempts would be different if the runner was on first as opposed to second. How they held the ball, their glove.

He studied no pitcher with more seriousness than the crafty Cy Young. Young always kept runners close, staring them back to the base. Cobb watched the great man closely; holding his glove near his chin sometimes, and at other times, lower on his chest when he planned a pickoff. With this knowledge, Ty was able easily to steal second.

Despite Young's declining years, Cobb, when asked about who was the greatest pitcher he ever faced, he said, "Aside from Walter Johnson, the old-timer Cy. "I think he is pitching as good today, as he did twenty years ago, even though I never faced him then." Ty said.

In the early fifties, Cobb attended induction ceremonies at the Hall of Fame. He was an honored guest in 1953 where he met Cy Young, who would pass away two years later.[29]

Cobb in Havana, Cuba

Cobb agreed, along with his teammates, to tour Havana, Cuba and play a twelve-game series against several teams, after the 1910 season was over. Although he missed the first several games, he arrived in late November to help the Tigers win 4-0.

---

[29] Don Rhodes, *Ty Cobb: Safe At Home* (Guilford, CT: Lyons Press, 2008).

Cobb attracted huge crowds helping the Tigers win seven games of the twelve played, one game ending in a tie. He said of the Cuban players: "They played good ball."[30]

Several Negro players went with the team, but played on the Cuban teams, as baseball in America was segregated. A star pitcher on one of the Cuban teams held Cobb to a single, and struck him out once. Cobb hit .370 in the five games he played.

Cobb said he had a lot of problems running the bases. On two attempts to steal second, the star black catcher, Juan Pedway, threw him out. He was upset at being thrown out by a black catcher' and vowed never to return to Cuba again. Possibly because of outstanding play of the black players on the Cuban team.

Other teams that played in Cuba were the Philadelphia Athletics in 1910 and 1911 followed by the New York Giants. In 1947, the Brooklyn Dodgers with Jackie Robinson played twenty-two exhibition games in Havana, winning 14, and losing 5, with 3 ties. On March 28, 1999, the Baltimore Orioles played an exhibition game in Havana. This was the first time a Major League team played in Cuba since 1959.

United States and Cuba Resume Relations

In late 2015, thanks to an agreement between President Barack Obama and President Raul Castro, the two countries resumed relations, ending a fifty-year ban and opened Embassies in Washington and Havana.

Numerous star Cuban players are currently playing in the Majors.[31] Thus MLB executives and some Minor League

---

[30] Hornbaker, *War on the Basepaths* ,118.
[31] A few of the Cuban players currently playing are Rusney Castillo, Boston Red Sox, Jose Abreu, Chicago White Sox, Jose Contreras, ex NY Yankees, Philadelphia

executives have held meetings to consider a Cuban team to join the International League.

Sources tell me, "The Cohen group, led by ex-Secretary of Defense under President Clinton, William Cohen is involved in trying to build bridges and eventually bring a franchise to Havana. This will be difficult to do due to the economic conditions in Cuba. The ballpark, that holds 50,000 was built in 1946 is antiquated and would require millions of dollars to bring it up to Organized Baseball requirements." Cohen said. In addition, the new administration under President Trump may have other ideas about Cuba.

Elvis Presley and Ty Cobb

It was the early fifties when Cobb was in Memphis, Tennessee on business. Some friends took him to a concert where he saw a talented young lad who sang and moved like no singer Ty had ever seen. It was Elvis Presley in the early days of his famous career. "The girls screamed their heads off," Ty said.

When introduced to Elvis, Cobb exclaimed: "Elvis, I believe you are going to make it big."

Cobb later commented to his friends, "I saw something I had never seen in the South before. Young white boys and girls, young colored boys and girls were sitting together, all mixed up, enjoying the music and having fun." That was against the rules in the South in those days. Segregation was the law. Elvis wouldn't play the concert any other way.

Cobb declared, "I told my friends I believe that music and Elvis Presley would help change the culture of America."

Phillies, Yoenis Cespedes, New York Mets, Aroldis Chapman, New York Yankees and Yasiel Puig, Los Angeles Dodgers.

Unusual Cobb fact: On July 15, 1924, while playing centerfield for Detroit against the Athletics, Ty had an unassisted double play.

Quotes about Cobb: Casey Stengel said, "Cobb once asked me what I thought was the most important position in baseball. I said, catcher, otherwise you would have a lot of passed balls."

Cobb quote:
"Two of the greatest pitchers I ever knew were Walter Johnson of the Washington Senators for his speed and Christy Mathewson of the New York Giants for his control and a breaking pitch that left batters helpless."

CHAPTER TWELVE
Cobb and Racism

Cobb Quotes:
"I clearly saw myself playing baseball in those Northern ballparks, and I saw myself a success"

C obb was often accused of being a racist, having been born in rural Georgia twenty-three years after the War Between the States. Several books written about Cobb accused him of being a racist without proof, probably due to his arguments and fights with black men.

One could say he was an equal opportunity fighter, as he had many arguments and fights with white men. Ty also fought with his teammates and others who rubbed him the wrong way. He had a thin skin and a viral nature, as even he admitted.

Ty became the poster child for racism as though he was the only man in baseball who was a racist. Many ballplayers and owners of the teams were racists, as well as the Commissioner of baseball, Kenneth Mountain Landis, who once said, "No Negro will ever play Major League baseball as long as I am Commissioner."

There was as much hatred, prejudice and discrimination of the coloreds in Boston, New York and California as there was in Mobile, Alabama, Memphis, Tennessee, Atlanta, Georgia, and Jackson, Mississippi. Many folk in the South loathed the hypocritical thinking of Northerners who closed their eyes to the discrimination or prejudice in the North.

It was against the rules of Major League baseball for Negroes to play on the same field with white players. The United States military was segregated during World War Two, which makes America, the bastion of freedom, look hypocritical, while the United States was fighting for liberty, freedom and democracy through Europe and Asia. It wasn't until after the War that President Harry Truman, by executive order integrated the military with Executive Order 9981. Issued on July 26, 1948, it abolished racial discrimination in the United States Armed Forces and eventually led to the end of segregation in the services.

At the turn of the 20th century and throughout the thirties, forties and fifties, whites considered blacks inferior in team sports, especially baseball. Black athletes were invisible in baseball, due to the rules of the game and the bigotry of many owners of the teams.

This was due to the racism that existed in American culture in parts of the North and in the South. The theory was, since no black players played baseball, ergo, they weren't intelligent enough to play the game, though no one doubted the physical capabilities of African/American athletes.[32]

Cobb could be disagreeable, touchy and aggressive at times, but he was one of the earliest supporters of integrating baseball.

---

[32] Jesse Owens won four gold medals in the 1936 Olympics in Berlin, Germany.

Ken Burns, one of America's premier documentarians got it wrong in his "Baseball" documentary when he called Cobb, "An embarrassment to baseball."

In the 1920s, Cobb befriended Negro League ballplayers such as Detroit star infielder Bobby Robinson. Robinson played in the Negro Leagues on five different teams and was known as the "Human Vacuum Cleaner" because of his fielding ability at third base. Robinson played with fellow Negro league player Satchel Paige. Robinson said: "There wasn't a hint of prejudice in Cobb's attitude."[33]

Alex Rivers was one of several blacks employed by Ty Cobb. He worked for Cobb for seven years until oil was discovered on land he owned in Mississippi, and became a millionaire. Rivers named his son after the Cobb and said, "I love the man."

Ball Boys on teams were brutally treated by players in the early days of the game. Cobb befriended a sixteen-year-old Negro mascot. Cobb defended the boy, and brought him on board a segregated train and let him sleep below his berth, hiding him from his teammates and passengers. He shared his room with the lad in segregated hotels.

At the end of the season, he brought the boy to his hometown of Royston, Georgia, and helped him get a job as a driver for a local businessman.[34]

Many of the sources of myths and lies told about Cobb came from a book written by Al Stump and the 1994 film, Cobb, starring Tommy Lee Jones. The script for the film came from Mr. Stump's book.

---

[33] Robinson retired from baseball in 1942. He died on May 17, 2002.

[34] Charles Leerhsen, Ty Cobb, *A Terrible Beauty* (New York: Simon & Schuster, 2015), 96

Ron Shelton, the director of Cobb allegedly told Mr. Leerhsen that it was "well known" that Cobb murdered three Negroes in Cleveland and raped a young woman in Las Vegas.[35]

After much fact checking by Leerhsen, he discovered there was never any press in Detroit or Las Vegas to substantiate the lies printed in the press. When Charles asked Ron where he got his facts from, Ron simply replied, "Everyone knows that."

Jackie Robinson Breaks the Color Barrier in 1947

Due to the foresight and inspiration of the Brooklyn Dodgers Branch Rickey, General Manager of the Dodgers, and the Commissioner of baseball, Colonel Albert "Happy" Chandler, baseball was integrated on April 15, 1947 when Jackie Robinson stepped onto the green grass at Ebbets Field.

So powerful was the grip of racism in America that no one questioned the logic of the belief that black athletes could not compete with whites. Jackie Robinson and all the African/American players that followed Jackie proved the absurdity of the kind of thinking that led people to believe that African Americans lacked intelligence to play baseball. The amazing Jesse Owens disproved much of that thinking in Germany in 1936 to the dismay of Adolf Hitler when he won four gold medals in the Berlin Olympics.

Oscar McKinley Charleston was often called, "The black Ty Cobb." He had the intensity of Ty Cobb, the dignity of Joe DiMaggio and the dedication of Lou Gehrig. He was one of the great Negro League players. Oscar was elected into the Hall of Fame in 1976.

---

[35] Ibid.

"Charleston was a tremendous left-handed hitter who could also bunt, steal a hundred bases a year, and cover center field as well as anyone before him or since. "He was like Ty Cobb, Babe Ruth and Tris Speaker rolled into one," said Buck O'Neil

Due to the writings of Al Stump and the movie Cobb, starring Tommy Lee Jones, Cobb became the metaphor for baseball's racism. During the time Cobb played, his stubborn refusal to play with the "darkies" was rampant throughout baseball and legalized by the new Commissioner of Baseball, appointed by the bigots who owned the teams, Judge, Kenesaw Mountain Landis.

The Judge had a reputation for being a bigot, and following the orders of the owners of the clubs, vowed to "never let a colored boy play in the Majors while I am Commissioner," the judge said.

If Ty were born 30 years later, he may have changed his thinking, as many Southerners did during the civil rights era. Cobb "Saw the light" in later years. He often spoke of the remarkable work "The colored nurses did" that worked in the Cobb Memorial Hospital.

Little was done in Georgia to care for the health needs of poor African/Americans and poor white folk until Ty funded his Ty Cobb Healthcare System in Royston, Georgia. Outside of Ted Williams, not many athletes engaged in philanthropic work.

Ty appointed an African/American, Doctor Mr. J.B. Gilbert to insure that both poor white folk and Negroes received the best care available. Eventually, he became Chief of Staff at Cobb's Hospital.

In 1952, five years before the Tigers signed their first African/American ballplayer, Jake Wood Jr. Cobb approved of a decision by a team in the Texas League to sign Negro players.[36] He was quoted as saying, "It is OK for them to play. I see no reason why we shouldn't compete with colored athletes as long as they conduct themselves with politeness and gentility." Cobb, known for his aggressive on and off the field said.

As complicated and misunderstood as Ty was, he continues to live out his Karma as a racist despite his change of thinking later in life. This is due to misinformation and myths told about Ty down the years that many people today still believe. The gifted and charming man may have been his own worst enemy.

When Pete Rose, as he was approaching Ty's hit record, was asked by a reporter if he thought Cobb was watching him from Heaven. Rose said, "From what I heard, that's not where he's at." Rose eventually reached the milestone on September 11, 1985, at home with Montreal against the San Diego Padres with a looping single to left off Eric Show for his 4,192nd hit of his career breaking Ty Cobb's record of 4,191.

Rogers Hornsby and a Discussion on Racism

Hornsby's career batting average of .358 is second best in the history of Major League Baseball behind Cobb's .367.He was the only player to ever hit at least forty home runs and hit .400 or better in the same season. He was inducted into the Hall of Fame in 1942.

On a hunting trip in the Grand Tetons, Wyoming in the mid-twenties, a reporter asked Ty who was the best hitter in the

---

[36] Jacob "Jake" Wood Jr., an African American from Elizabeth, New Jersey, signed with the Detroit Tigers in 1957. He made his debut with the Tigers on April 11, 1961 against the Cleveland Indians. Hitting leadoff, the right-handed batter went 1-for-4, belting a two-run home run in the seventh inning.

Majors beside him. Ty said, "Hornsby of the St. Louis Cardinals, he could sure hit."

The Ku Klux Klan was America's leading terrorist organization, there isn't much competition in the game of hatred and discrimination; it wins that contest by a wide margin. The story of the KKK will tell you everything about the darker side of our country's history.[37]

Following the Civil War, the Ku Klux Klan emerged to suppress and victimize newly freed slaves. Founded in 1866, the Ku Klux Klan (KKK) extended into almost every southern state by 1870 and became a vehicle for white southern resistance to the Republican Party's Reconstruction. In his book: *"The New Bill James Historical Baseball Abstract,"* James notes: The KKK in the 1920's had a populist phase in which it toned down its racism, and drew in hundreds of thousands of men who were not racists, including Supreme Court Justice Hugo Black.

Baseball fans interested in history get upset about supposed racist Ty Cobb while generally ignoring the alleged KKK membership of Hall of Famers Tris Speaker and Rogers Hornsby. The point here is that KKK membership in the 1920s was not incompatible with being one of the most famous athletes in the country. Ty Cobb never joined the KKK.

Cobb attended the 1926 World Series managed by Rogers Hornsby. The Hornsby led Cardinals beat the Babe Ruth led Yankees, 4-3. Cobb and Hornsby celebrated the Cardinals victory with several drinks. The two southerners, Rogers from Winters Texas, and Cobb, from Georgia, got into a discussion about the Civil War. A joyous Hornsby, with too many drinks under his belt, explained the southern point of view of the loss of the war.

---

[37] Eric Foner's Reconstruction: America's Unfinished Revolution 1863-1877

Hornsby, slurring his words told Ty, "We didn't lose the war! We were outnumbered and outgunned. That good ole boy, General Lee surrendered to General Grant at Appomattox in April 1965. We let the Yankees think they won. Old Abe Lincoln may have freed the slaves with his Emancipation Proclamation, but we kept the Negro in his place for the next sixty years."

Hornsby continued his oration that reflected the thinking of many Southerners. "The coloreds couldn't vote, couldn't go to our churches or attend our schools. They couldn't eat in our restaurants, or drink from our water fountains. They couldn't pee in our bathrooms, attend our libraries, or swim in our public pools." Hornsby proudly said.

"When they went to our movies, we made 'em sit in the highest balcony. We called it Negro heaven. When they rode our buses, we made 'em sit in the back. If they got uppity, or looked at our women wrong, we strung 'em up from the highest tree." Hornsby laughed.

Cobb said, "Good night Rogers," and left the bar.

Cobb Accused of Gambling

Hubert Benjamin (Dutch) Leonard was a pitcher for the Detroit Tigers and had many reasons to accuse Ty Cobb and Tris Speaker of gambling. He disagreed with how manager Ty Cobb handled him and he strongly believed both Cobb and Speaker "railroaded" him out of baseball, so and he sought his revenge.

He had acquired a reputation for being a whiner, and Cobb never liked his negative attitude. Dutch complained Ty, as manager overworked him. He thought Tris Speaker, manager of the Cleveland Indians would sign him after the Tigers waived him. Speaker wanted no part of him. Thus Leonard was convinced the two men conspired to drive him out of baseball.

Leonard wrote letters to Commissioner Landis accusing both men of gambling. The year was 1925 and the World Series gambling scandal in 1919 was on Landis's mind. Cobb and Speaker demanded the Commissioner delve into the accusation. Both men requested Landis order Leonard to the Commissioner's office in New York and face both men and accuse them to their face,

Cobb said, "I wanted Dutch to tell me to my face, to look into my eyes to tell me I placed a bet. He never did face me. I called him "gutless" for refusing to accuse me in person." Later, in California where Dutch lived, he bragged to reporters saying, "I have had my revenge on Cobb and Speaker."

At a hearing in Landis's office, over forty players from the White Sox and Tigers gave evidence about other gambling adventures. Baseball had a problem with gambling from the turn of the Century to the World Series scandal of 1919. Cobb said, "I called Landis and asked him to ask every player there if they ever knew that I gambled and to a man, they all swore under oath that I was honest and was innocent as well as Speaker."

Cobb did admit he became bitter toward Landis the way he handled the situation. Some people believe the reason Cobb missed the official photo of the first class inducted into the Hall of Fame in 1936 was not because he missed his train, but because it was his desire not to see Landis.

After the Commissioner found Cobb and Speaker not guilty of any charges, the Tigers released Cobb from his contract in early 1927. He signed a contract to play for Connie Mack's

Philadelphia Athletics and Tris Speaker signed with the Washington Senators.

Ty Cobb Was Not a Racist

Many books and numerous articles have been written about Ty Cobb. In 1994, the movie Cobb starring Tommy Lee Jones made an appearance to disastrous financial failure and was eventually removed from theaters.

Cobb's relationship with blacks and minorities is a mixed bag, depending on which authors one reads. Taking into account newspapers when Cobb played often played up the racial issue to sell newspapers. Some papers and sports reporters had their own built in biases against Negroes.

There is little evidence suggesting Cobb was a racist simply because he was born in Georgia in 1886. Cobb's father believed in public education for black Americans, and Ty spoke out for integration of baseball.

Cobb was reported to have fought two black men in a hotel in Cleveland.[38] In his book "Ty Cobb, A Terrible Beauty" author Charles Leershen through extensive research in old Detroit Free Press papers showed that a fight Cobb had in the hotel in Cleveland was with two white men. Much that has been written has been misinterpreted or totally false.

Much negativity about Ty came about after he died in July 1961. Al Stump, a writer that Cobb hired to write his biography painted Cobb in a fair light in his first book, *My Life in Baseball.* However, his second book, written about thirty years later, (*Cobb: The Life and Times of the Meanest Man in Baseball*), painted an extremely negative view of the man, with many stories that

---

[38] Alexander, *Ty Cobb*

Cobb allegedly told Stump, with no verification and portrayed Cobb as a racist.

Stump claimed Ty murdered three black men in Cleveland and raped a white woman in Las Vegas. These accusations are false and have long since been repudiated.

In the late 1920's Cobb leased a hunting preserve with over 12,000 acres in Magruder, Georgia and built a house on it for a black man named Uncle Bob Robinson and his family to live there.

Cobb hunted there many times with friends and always invited Mr. Robinson to hunt with the group.

In 1908, Cobb bought fifteen acres in Toccoa, Georgia, a predominantly black neighborhood. He built many small but attractive homes for the Negros. He called the subdivision, "Booker T. Washington Heights" and leased the homes for a minimal amount.

One of Cobb's fondest memories of his youth was of being taught how to swim by a black laborer named Uncle Ezra. Ezra would get young Ty to cling to his neck and wade out into the middle of the river or stream. At this point, Ty would be released and forced to swim back to the riverbank.

An article about Cobb appeared in the Independent Journal, Menlo Park, California dated January 29, 1952 stating that, "Tyrus Raymond Cobb, fiery old-time star of the diamond, stepped up to the plate today to clout a verbal home run in favor of Negroes in baseball. Cobb, a native of the Deep South voiced approval of the recent decision of a Dallas, Texas club to use "Negro players if they came up to Texas league caliber."

He spoke emphatically on the subject of Negroes in baseball. "Certainly it is O.K. for them to play. I see no reason in the world why we shouldn't compete with colored athlete." Cobb stated.

Cobb, referring again to developments in the Texas league declared, *"It was bound to come."* He meant the breaking down of baseball's racial barriers in the old south. Cobb expressed the belief Negroes eventually would be playing in every league in the country

Ty Cobb was a close associate to the second commissioner of baseball, Colonel Albert B. "Happy" Chandler from Kentucky. "Happy" was head of the baseball realm when Jackie Robinson entered into Major League Baseball in 1947.

Cobb, in a press interview on August 30, 1950, shared his support for Chandler, "So far, Chandler has lived up to everything that I thought he could do as a Commissioner. To me, every one of his decisions has been fair."

He expressed his thoughts about ending segregation in baseball to the Commissioner by saying, "It is time to end segregation in baseball; that was a lousy rule."

The article goes on explaining Cobb's support for "Happy." Three years later, he was elected to serve as member of the Board of Trustees of the Cobb Educational Foundation.

In 1953, Cobb established the Ty Cobb Educational Foundation to give scholarships to needy students in Georgia, regardless of race. Hundreds of young black students have become a beneficiary of this educational fund.

"Ty Cobb was not a racist, he did not sharpen his spikes nor did he intentionally spike infielders or catchers, he did not kill a man in Detroit, as alleged by a few misinformed writers, and he did not live the life of a bigot. Contrary to those myths, Cobb exerted a kindness toward African-Americans."[39]

Quotes about Cobb: "Cobb was always trying to mess with the mind of his opponents. He was always trying to rattle the other side anyway he could." Grantland Rice, sports writer

Cobb on base stealing: "Not even a home run with the bases loaded can demoralize an infield and get the defense up in the air like clever base running can do."

Cobb statistical records: Games played – 3033 (5th place)

---

[39] The author wishes to thank Wesley Fricks, Ty Cobb Historian, a man nationally recognized as an expert on Mr. Cobb. He helped establish the Ty Cobb Museum in Royston, Georgia. Fricks emphatically states in his book and writing that Cobb was not a racist.

CHAPTER THIRTEEN
Cobb on Base Running

Cobb quotes:
"Sliding is a marvelous art in baseball. A player has to have a certain flair for sliding. It has to come natural despite all the practice. Some players have the ability to contort or twist their bodies while flying through the air or sliding into the dirt. A player has to love this part of the game."

"The aggressive man and the man who has no fear of injury is the definition of a base runner. Infielders will attempt all kinds of schemes to prevent a player from reaching a base. Every ploy has been tried against me, but I beat them all." Ty said.

"Pay attention at all times," is my motto, Ty claimed. He then told the following story. "I was on second and the batter hit a hot grounder to third. The third baseman fired the ball to first and I rounded third and took a lead toward home. The first baseman faked a throw to third, then fired the ball there to catch me off base, but I raced home and scored," Ty laughed, outsmarting the first baseman, Hal Chase.

"I had seen Chase do that many times so I knew he would try to catch me. But, I was savvy to his plan, and I outfoxed him. By always paying attention to what seems like minor details, by studying the mannerisms of all fielders and outfielders, it will help you in the future." Ty cracked up pleased as punch telling the story to a reporter

The Master's advice on sliding was to complete the slide for each attempt. If at the last second the runner, racing at full speed changes his mind, he is apt to break or sprain an ankle. It would be disastrous for the runner to change his mind at the last second because he thought there was no play to be made at the base.

An iconic photo of Cobb sliding into third base. This is one of baseball's most famous photos, and hangs in the Hall of Fame.

"Once I made up my mind to hit the dirt, I never changed it, and came in at full speed. This is the safest and best way. Never slide in head first - you're asking for a spiking on your fingers, arms or back," Cobb said.

He talked about his first attempt to steal second. "I slid in head first. The shortstop slapped my head hard with his glove, stomped on my back and threw dirt in my eyes. I heard the umpire yell: 'You're out!' I got up bleeding all over, with dirt in my eyes. Sliding in head first is dumb and I never did that again," he said.[40]

Cobb mastered the art of the fade away, always sliding away from where the fielder's eyes told him where the ball was coming, giving the fielder only the tip of the shoe to tag as he slid around the base.

He proved that baseball is a game of the mind as well as the body, by keeping detailed notes on the pitching motions of every pitcher. By studying every move the pitcher makes, toward first, or to home, it could mean an extra six or seven steals for him over a season.

"Every pitcher has a different move. Pay attention!" Ty repeats. "Watch the pitchers hip movement, knee, foot or shoulder, that shows what the pitcher is about to do." Cobb reiterates.

"Always keep your eye on the ball. Pitchers will hide the ball in their glove, or behind their back. You will see it at the last split second and you may get a clue what the next pitch will be, if you study the pitchers movements." he said.

In today's game, players study video. In Cobb's day, he was known as a great note taker. He would mentally record notes, and then sit in his hotel room transcribing his notes to a pad while his teammates were out drinking beer. It was the brain part of the game, the hours he spent studying his notes, and dreaming up plays that would confuse his opponents that made Ty the outstanding performer he was.

"Baseball is a game of the mind, as well as the body, brains as well as brawn," Cobb remarked.

---

[40] Cobb kept the headfirst slide in his bag of sliding tricks to be used when he deemed it proper and safe.

Ty recommended the runner watch the eyes of the infielder. When racing at full speed down the line, one should not turn his head to look at the outfielder. You will lose a second he said, and every second counts. The fielder's eyes tell the runner if the ball is coming in high to the left. If so, then slide to the right of the base. If the ball is coming in low, to the right, slide to the left he advised. You can do this if you study the eyes of the fielder as you approach the base.

This is one of Ty's ploys that he perfected when he was on first. He would flash a bunt sign to the hitter, who had to be an excellent bunter to make this work. The batter would bunt to third, as Ty roared around second. The third baseman, would rush forward to field the bunt, throw to first, then rush back to third too late, as Ty slid in safely.

Ty, like many creative artists or inventors believed his best baseball ideas came to him at night, just before going to sleep. He would get up; and write them down in his notebook.

Spikes & Spiking

Spikes and spiking are as old as baseball. Players who retire from the game - whether high school, college, the minors or majors - treasure their uniforms, caps and gloves, but most of all, their spikes.

Spikes help the runner, but also can be used to intimidate an opponent. The myth about Cobb is he had a reputation for sharpening his spikes and spiking infielders as he slid in. This is one of the many myths about Ty. He maintained that he never sharpened his spikes. Cobb said: "I never intentionally spiked an infielder, unless he played sloppy or clumsy or tried to block the base on me. The base paths belong to me. If they were spiked, it was their fault." Cobb said.

He also said, "Sportswriters never wrote about how many times I was spiked. I have more scars on my ankles, legs, arms, thighs and back, than Babe Ruth hit home runs but most of the spikings were unintentional. There is a lot of jumping around when a player slides in, and the fielder is also jumping around."

When Enos Slaughter spiked Jackie Robinson in St. Louis in 1947 while Jackie was playing first, it was seen as deliberate and an act of racism. Slaughter always denied that.

When Ty played, baseball shoes had two separate triangular metal plates attached, one to the heel and one to the toe or front part of the shoe. This triangle metal plate had three metal cleats, or spikes. Each spike or cleat was about 1/2 or 5/8 inches in width and length.

Modern design and construction of baseball playing shoes are now more commonly a one-piece molded rubber or other synthetic material that provides blinding speed traction.

During the course of playing many games, these spikes would wear down and become flat or dull. Players wanted as much digging or bite into the ground as possible to improve their traction and speed. Many players would sharpen these spikes with the use of a file provided by the clubhouse manager.

For hard-nosed players, "Take no prisoners," was a phrase used by many players. This was an act of sharpening their spikes to serve as an ulterior motive other than adding speed. Ty Cobb was known throughout the game as a no holds barred fierce competitor. He denied spiking anyone intentionally as he wanted players to believe he would spike them.

It was his way of intimidating the opponent, of planting fear in their mind. The smart fielder would stand off the base allowing Cobb a clear path to the bag. He called this, "My patch, stay out of my patch and you won't be spiked. If you get spiked, it would be your fault," Cobb reiterated.

Spiking infielders in today's game is not considered a part of the macho, tough, fierce, fight-em-hard spread fear, like in days past.

When a runner attempts to break up a double play at second, bad things can happen as it did in the seventh inning of Game 2 of the NLCS playoff game in 2015 between the Dodgers and Mets won by the Dodgers 5-2.

Howie Kendrick hit a ground ball up the middle, and second baseman Daniel Murphy fed the ball to shortstop Ruben Tejada for a potential double play. That was never turned. It wasn't even attempted. Chase Utley upended Tejada at second base with a brutal take-out slide.

Utley is a second baseman, and he's been on the wrong end of take-out slides many times during his career. Utley could take it and dished it out with the best of them.

Tejada, meanwhile, had to be carted off the field after the take-out slide. His right leg was stabilized. The Mets later announced he suffered a fractured right fibula on the play. Tejada was done for the series.

Cobb was involved in a controversial spiking of Frank Baker of the Philadelphia Athletics on August 24, 1909. Cobb was on second and took off for third. The catcher's throw to Baker had Ty easily beat but when Baker tried to tag Ty, his foot flashed out and hit Baker's forearm drawing blood.

Although Cobb was called a dirty player for this incident, Philadelphia fans and Philly media never forgave him for that incident. A photo showed Baker leaning over the bag and the league president Ban Johnson said Ty was in his rights.

Baker wasn't hurt, and years later both men would laugh about the scandal the Philadelphia reporters made of the incident.[41]

Quotes about Cobb: "Cobb is a great ball player, one of the greatest I ever saw. Cobb is a fine fellow." Honus Wagner - Pittsburgh Pirates, Hall of Famer.

Cobb on base stealing: "Take advantage of a slow fielding outfielder by converting a single to a double. You may get away with taking the extra base or the fielder in his haste to nail you, may throw the ball away."

Cobb statistical records: Prolific Hitters – Cobb is 7th on a list of 11 players who hit over 240 hits in a season.

---

[41] Bak, *Peach*

CHAPTER FOURTEEN
Captain Cobb – U. S. Army

Cobb quotes:
"I was always trying to rattle the other side any way I could, at the plate or on the base paths."

World War I was raging in Europe, and the 1918 season was shortened. Cobb hit .384 and won his eleventh batting title. The Tigers were playing in Washington in mid-August and Ty paid a visit to his friend in the White House, President Woodrow Wilson.

Shortly after New Year's Day 1918, Cobb expressed his interest to join the Marine Corps. Being subject to the draft and slightly missing the draft the previous year, friends of Cobb believed that he would secure a place in the Army or Navy before the draft could catch up with him.

The following week, January 24th, Cobb was reclassified because he had a wife and three children that were dependent upon him. The deferred rating resulted from parental dependency that placed him back in class two. On April 24th, while on a road trip in Cleveland, Ty helped his younger brother Paul enlist and join the Marine Corps, where he was immediately dispatched to Paris Island, South Carolina for training.

By the middle of July Cobb was ready to join the Army. "I felt angry every time I look at a casualty list and want to go to Europe and kill some Germans." Cobb said.

When the United States entered into World War I, many players enlisted in the Army, as Cobb did in August 1918. Shoeless Joe Jackson was a married man and was granted a deferment by his hometown draft board in Greenville, South Carolina.

"Though I am in a deferred class because I have a wife and three children, I feel that I must give up baseball because of my patriotic feelings at the close of the season and do my duty for my country in the best way possible." Cobb said.

On August 17, 1918, Ty Cobb took his test for commission in the Gas and Flame Division for the United States Army and was pronounced in perfect condition in every aspect.

Although President Wilson was born and raised in Staunton, Virginia, he and Ty became friends when, while Governor of New Jersey in 1910, the Governor visited his hometown of Augusta, Georgia where Wilson had lived. Ty lived with his family in Augusta and took great pride in giving Mr. Wilson a private tour of the city.

President Wilson thanked him for being a leader in getting ball players to join the military. The season ended in August that year and many other players joined forces with other civilians in the "War to end all wars" as the president called it.

Ty said, "Mr. President, I wholeheartedly approve of your decision to declare war on Germany and I believe it is my patriotic duty to serve my country."

The President shook his hand saying he appreciated his patriotism. Ty promptly joined the Chemical Warfare Service. On August 28th, the War Department announced the appointment of Tyrus Raymond Cobb to the Chemical Warfare Service of the U. S. Army, and was commissioned Captain.

The 1918 season was shortened due to the war. Cobb hit .384 winning his 11th batting title.

Cobb was not the only athlete to be commissioned to the Army's Chemical Division. Christy Mathewson, pitcher for the New York Giants; Branch Rickey, president of the St. Louis Cardinals and many others also joined the CWS.

He departed in early September and arrived in Claumont, France in mid-September where he trained soldiers in the correct use of their gas masks. Cobb served sixty-seven days in France training Allied Forces to prepare for chemical attacks.

Cobb never did see any action, but had just completed his training at the American General Headquarters when the armistice was signed. However, during a training exercise at a gas school in Chaumont, some gas was released before the officers in charge gave out the go-ahead.

Christy Mathewson, star pitcher for the New York Giants also a Captain was part of that exercise. Mathewson and Cobb received a full dose of the poisonous gas before strapping on their gas mask and helping the other CWS troops to safety.

Cobb coughed up green fluid for months but Mathewson's dose was believed to be the cause of the tuberculosis that took the star's life several years later in 1925.

Cobb on the Set - Gone With the Wind

Gone With the Wind (1939) is often considered the most beloved, enduring and popular film of all time.

Cobb had long retired from baseball but he was a celebrity that other famous celebrities liked being around him. He was invited to the set when the movie starring Clark Gable and Vivien Leigh was being filmed. Clark Gable was a Hollywood star and famed British born Vivien Leigh played the indomitable heroine, Scarlett O'Hara.

Despite being British, Vivien played the role of a Southern Belle, Scarlett with delightful charm, as though she was born in the South and raised on a plantation in Atlanta. Her performance won her an Oscar.

Cobb said, "I fell madly in love with Vivien but she was married to that great British actor, Lawrence Olivier. And of course, I was married too." Ty declared.

Cobb on hitting

Cobb always maintained he was not a natural-born hitter. "There is no such thing, just as there are no natural born singers, dancers, pianists or writers. It comes with determination to succeed, and practice, practice, practice." Cobb often said.

Ty with his famous hands-apart batting grip

"The Lord blessed me with great eyesight and quick reflexes," Ty stated. He pointed out that Ted Williams' eyesight was 10/10. That and Ted's incredible reflexes led him to become a great hitter and expert jet pilot during WWII and the Korean War.

Ty strongly believed in taking good care of ones' eyes. He said: "I avoided reading in poor light, watching many movies and get lots of rest," was the advice he gave hitters. Ty also believed smoking and drinking alcohol were injuries to one health.

Cobb's advice to youngsters who wish to become good hitters was, "To become a student of hitting, you can't be afraid of getting hit by a pitch. When pitchers discover the batter backs away from inside pitchers, pitchers will continue to pitch closer and closer until they drive the hitter out of the game" he strongly believed.

"It takes a strong heart, with no fear to become a good hitter and a good mind, to know what pitch to hit, and which to lay off. Great hitters learn to avoid the bad ball. If they don't, pitchers will continue to give that hitter bad balls to swing at." Ty stressed.

Cobb's Rules and Suggestions for Hitters

Cobb was a master hitting coach. Lefty O'Doul and Harry Heilman are prime examples of hitters who became great thanks to Cobb's instructions. The following are some basic rules Cobb gave to his students:

"Develop your own style of hitting; avoid copying the style of great sluggers you admire. Their style may not work for you. Don't try to smash the ball as though trying for a home run. When a pitcher throws a curve, don't back away. If you do, pitchers will continue to curve you."

"Always keep your eye on the ball the moment the pitcher receives it. Good pitchers will try to hide the ball, sometimes with eccentric motions. Don't listen to the catchers hitting instructions; he is trying to fool you."

"Be aware of your own faults, work on improving them. Try to outguess the pitcher. If you accomplish this, you will own the pitcher for the day."

"Listen to your hitting coach - they know more than you do. Weak hitters have been known to become good hitters, by listening to their coach, and not being afraid to change their hitting style. Sometimes, a longer or shorter bat, or a heavier or lighter one could do the trick."

"Try moving to the back of the batter's box when you think a pitcher will throw a curve. You will have a better chance of hitting the ball.

"Have a positive frame of mind. Be happy, have fun. Most players hit better when they are loose and happy. Never swing at a bad ball. This is a cardinal sin for hitters. Wait for your pitch."

"Pay attention to where the fielders are playing. Try a bluff to third when he comes in. Then bang it past him. If the first or third baseman are playing in their normal positions, drag a bunt down the line, you will probably beat it out for a single."

"Pitchers pay attention to the batters feet. I would place my feet as though I was going to pull the ball to right field. The pitcher may throw outside, but I would change my feet, mid-pitch and bang the ball to left."

"The most foolish thing a batter can do is to try to smash the ball over the fence instead of hitting for the single or double, the home runs will come when you least expect it. This is called pressing and has ended the career of many a hitter; practice, practice, practice."

Quotes about Cobb: "The greatness of Ty Cobb was something that had to be seen." - George Sisler, Hall-of-Famer.

Cobb tips: "Pay attention to details. Make mental notes on pitchers, catchers and the fielders. Study their mannerisms. Write them in your notebook."

Cobb statistical records: Prolific Hitters: 11 players have hit over 240 hits in a season. Cobb ranks 7th with 248.

CHAPTER FIFTEEN
The Day the Tigers Went on Strike

Cobb Quotes:
"I took great pleasure in mentoring and helping a young Italian boy named Joe DiMaggio negotiate a more lucrative contract from the New York Yankees."

For the first time in baseball history, and the last time, a team went on strike and refused to play in support of Cobb. On May 15, 1912 in a game against the New York Highlanders in New York, a fan in the stands assaulted Cobb with foul, abusive and such vulgar language that Ty, with furious rage, leaped into the stands to punish the scurrilous rude fan.

This fan was disrespectful to all the Tigers, but he saved his most vile and derogatory remarks toward Cobb. Ty ignored the fan but when he called Ty a half N...a remark that no Southerner could tolerate, Cobb's Southern blood was boiling and he erupted like a broken boiler and jumped into the stands and began a punishing, brutal attack on the abuser.

The Tiger players also went into the stands, but made no attempt to restrain Ty, feeling it was useless. They stood by, and watched as juveniles might watch a brawl in high school. After Ty administered a "brutal thrashing" as one paper reported, the local police and players finally intervened and pulled Cobb off the beaten and bloodied fan.

The umpire threw Cobb out of the game and league president Ban Johnson suspended Cobb for ten games for "conduct unbecoming a gentleman."

Despite the animosity many Tiger players felt toward Ty, they rallied behind their teammate, demanding that Ty be reinstated...or else! They threatened not to play the next game in Philadelphia but President Johnson refused to be threatened, and did not lift the suspension or fine he levied on Cobb.

Facing a possible forfeit and a $5000.00 fine, Tiger manager Hughie Jennings put a call out for local college players to play a Major League game. Many came from the local college St. Joseph's College; a few high school seniors, old-timers, Tiger coaches also volunteered to play, and manager Jennings completed the lineup.

Placing this rag-tag group of men in the game would not produce a Major League lineup just as putting wings on dogs would not enable them to fly like birds. The game took place in Philadelphia at Shibe Park and the Athletics smashed the mixed bag of incompetent players, 24-2.[42]

The following day, the strike over, Cobb approached his teammates telling them he was touched by their solidarity in backing him. Cobb told them how much, "I appreciate what you did for me," and he urged them to suit up for the next

[42] Shibe Park, opened in 1901 was later known as Connie Mack Stadium. It was the home of the Philadelphia Athletics of the American League and the Philadelphia Phillies of the National League.

game or face fines and possible banishment from Major League baseball. The team played as Cobb suggested.[43]

The mixed bag of players who played for the Tigers that day were officially recognized as Major League players for one game.

Cobb and Shoeless Joe Jackson

Shoeless Joe Jackson took his shoes off his before an at-bat in Greenville, S.C., because the cleats he had been wearing were giving him blisters. That is how he acquired the nickname, "Shoeless Joe." His name remains very much alive in the minds of baseball fans, in part because of the 1919 Black Sox Scandal that cost him his career, and in part because of that indelible nickname.

The Black Sox Scandal was a Major League Baseball match fixing incident in which eight members of the Chicago White Sox were accused of intentionally losing the 1919 World Series against the Cincinnati Reds. On October 9, 1919, the Cincinnati Reds defeated the heavily favored Chicago White 10-5 to clinch an unlikely World Series win. Prior to the start of the Series, rumors were spread that before the first pitch was thrown, gamblers had paid several White Sox players to intentionally lose games. Jackson was one of eight men accused of taking part in the plot.

Joe acquired the nickname Shoeless Joe by a reporter in the *Greenville South Carolina News*. He allegedly played a game in his stocking feet because his new baseball shoes were not yet broken in, or as Joe said, "They gave me blisters." For the rest of his life he was known as Shoeless Joe Jackson.

---

[43] Bert Randolph Sugar, *Baseball's 50 Greatest Games* (New York, Simon & Schuster, 1987), 180

He didn't like his nickname and later told a reporter, "I've read and heard every kind of yarn imaginable on how I got the name. I never played the outfield barefoot, and that was the only day I ever played in my stocking feet, but it stuck with me."

The book and film "Eight Men Out" explains in detail the story of the scandal that shocked America and brought Federal Judge Kennesaw Mountain Landis to become baseball's first Commissioner. The headlines proclaimed the 1919 fix of the World Series attempted a cover-up as "The most gigantic sporting swindle in the history of America!" First published in 1963, "Eight Men Out" has become a timeless classic. The book reconstructs the entire scene-by-scene story of the fantastic scandal in which eight Chicago White Sox players arranged with the nation's leading gamblers to throw the Series to Cincinnati. The film was released September 2, 1988.

Joseph Jefferson Wofford "Shoeless Joe" Jackson was born on July 16, 1888, in rural Pickens County, South Carolina. He is most famous, or infamous for being one of eight players on the Chicago White Sox who were accused of throwing the World Series to the Cincinnati Reds in 1919. The event became known as the Black Sox Scandal.[44]

Cobb hailed Jackson as one the greatest natural hitters in the history of the game. He was a powerful man famed for his line drives to all parts of the field. He led the American League in triples three times. Joe never won a batting title, but his average of .408 in 1911 still stands as a Cleveland team record and a major-league rookie record. Cobb batted .420 that year to win the batting title.

---

[44] Information on Jackson appeared in "Scandal on the South Side: The 1919 Chicago White Sox." Also, "Deadball Stars of the American League" (Potomac Books, 2006). Harvey Frommer, "Shoeless Joe and Ragtime Baseball." (Dallas Taylor Publishing, 1992)

After Jackson hit .408 in 1911 and failed to win the batting title, he griped to a reporter saying, "What a hell of a league this is. I hit .387, .408, and .395 the last three years and I ain't won nothin' yet! That's because Cobb beat me all three times!"[45]

Jackson named his bat Black Betsy. It was thirty-six inches long and weighed forty-eight ounces. Ty also said, "Joe was the best slugger I ever saw until Ruth. Most of us punched at the ball. Not Joe. He swung the bat harder than we did and he hit it on a line. Ruth told me he copied Jackson's swing."

Babe Ruth said of Joe, "I copied Jackson's style because I thought he was the greatest natural hitter I had ever seen. He's the guy who made me a hitter." Joe became a star in 1911 battering American League pitching for 233 hits, 45 doubles, 19 triples, and a .408 batting average.

Cobb used the hands-apart-on-the-bat approach, but Joe put his hands together near the bottom of the handle, and took a full swing. He stood deep in the box, feet close together, then took one long step into the pitch and ripped at it with his left-handed swing. Babe said, "I copied my swing after Joe Jackson's. His swing was perfect."

The Indians Traded Joe to the Chicago White Sox in 1915

Joe helped the unhappy White Sox team win the pennant in 1919, finishing fourth in the league in batting with a .351. The talented White Sox were heavily favored to win the nine games World Series. But many of the Sox players were disgruntled by the way owner Charles Comiskey dismissed their requests for higher salary.

---

[45] Douglass Wallop, *Baseball; an informal history*– (New York: W.W. Norton & Co, 1969)

New York gamblers offered Chick Gandil $10.000. Gandil then approached Jackson with a large offer. Joe declined, and Gandil offered $20.000, three times Jackson's annual salary. Again, Joe said no. Arnold Rothstein, a big time New York gambler may have been a major player in the scandal but his involvement was never proven. Chick Gandil and his co-conspirators were considered the leaders in the plot.

Joe's participation consisted solely of trusting Gandil, a stunning amount of faith in a man whom he didn't know very well. It was an incredible lapse of judgment, as well as a failure of character, on Jackson's part.

Jackson, who ultimately received only $500.00 batted .375 against the Reds and did his best to help the Sox win, to no avail. Jackson had no formal education, and could neither read nor write. When a gambler asked Joe to sign a paper proffering $500.00, Joe signed his name with an X.

Cincinnati defeated the favored White Sox, winning its first World Series title. Jackson tied a record with his 12 hits in the Series. Despite taking the money, Joe did his best to help his team win.

The following season 1920, Joe signed for a substantial raise, a three-year deal for $8,000 per year. Jackson gave one of his finest performances in 1920, with a .382 average, a career-best 121 runs batted in, and a league-leading 20 triples.

Word was spreading in the media that eight players including Jackson helped throw the Series. Due to wide spread gambling in baseball, the owners, led by Mr. Comiskey hired a Federal Judge, Kennesaw Mountain Landis, and gave him full power to handle the problem. Comiskey also hired a private detective to look into the affair.

Despite being acquitted by a jury of their peers in court in Chicago, all eight accused players, including the retired Gandil, were eventually banished from baseball for life by new Commissioner Landis. The scandal brought a sad and untimely end to Joe Jackson's brilliant baseball career. Banned from baseball for life, the fight to have Joe reinstated and admitted to the Hall of Fame still rages on.

Jackson, whose lifetime batting average of .356 is the third highest in the game's history behind Cobb at .367 and Rogers Hornsby at .358 was not admitted into the Hall of Fame.

Cobb was a long-time admirer of the talent of Jackson. Ty thought highly of Jackson believing he got a bad deal in the Black Sox scandal of 1919. Cobb said, "Joe wasn't the brightest bulb in the barrel, but he could sure hit."

Ted William once remarked, "When I was younger, the Red Sox used to play an exhibition game in Greenville, South Carolina where Joe lived. He was still alive. Oh how I wish I had known that. I would have stopped in and talk hitting with that man." Ted said.

Many years later, Ty and his friend Grantland Rice paid a visit to Joe who owned a liquor store in Greenville, South Carolina. The two men walked into the shop and ordered several bottles of whisky.[46]

"What's the matter with you Joe, don't you remember me?" Cobb asked Joe. "Of course I do Ty, but I thought you wouldn't want to talk to me," Joe said.

---

[46] Henry Grantland Rice was an early 20th-century American sportswriter known for his elegant prose. His writing was published in newspapers around the country and broadcast on the radio.

In those days, players did not have pensions or social security. Cobb financially supported numerous players, including Joe and his family when Joe was in poor health towards the end of his life. Cobb had a business associate handle the transactions. Recipients of the hard cash never knew it was Cobb who provided the money.

Jackson suffered a heart attack and died at home at the age of 63, on December 5, 1951. He was buried in Woodlawn Memorial Park in Greenville, South Carolina. The Shoeless Joe Jackson Museum is located in Greenville.[47]

Sam (Wahoo) Crawford

Sam Crawford began his baseball career playing semi-pro ball around his birthplace of Wahoo, Nebraska, hence the nickname, "Wahoo Sam"

Sam started his major league career with Cincinnati but joined the Tigers in 1903; he retired in 1917, playing the balance of his career with the Tigers.

He batted left-handed and led the league in triples six times, finishing with an all-time record of .309 that will probably never be broken. This record is 90 years old. His 56 inside-the-park home runs is still the best in baseball.

The Tiger teams of 1907-09 led by Ty Cobb and Crawford made three consecutive World Series appearances, but lost all three.

Unlike Cobb, Crawford refrained from the science approach to the game that Cobb employed so well. Crawford's approach to success was seeing the ball he liked, and hitting it as hard as he could. Crawford was a leading slugger for the Tiger from

---

[47] The mailing address for the Museum is 4755, Greenville, SC 29608.

1904-07 until Cobb joined the team winning nine consecutive batting titles and replacing Sam as a super star.

Cobb felt Sam was jealous of his success, causing a rift between the two great players. Sam believed Ty had an "antagonistic attitude."

He told a reporter that: "Cobb came up from the South, and he was still fighting the Civil War. As far as he was concerned, we were all damn Yankees before he even met us. Sure we hazed him like we did all rookies; most could take it, but not Cobb. He turned it into a life or death struggle."[48]

The young Ty met Sam Crawford during an exhibition game in Augusta when Crawford's Tigers played Cobb's Augusta Tourists in 1904. Cobb gingerly approached Sam, asking him for some advice. Sam said, "Don't drink on game days." One year later, they were both playing for the Tigers.

Despite the many feuds the two men had when they played, it was Ty Cobb who was instrumental in getting Sam Crawford into the Hall of Fame. Ty was a vociferous letter writer, and wrote to many influential people on Crawford's behalf. The Veterans Committee inducted Crawford into the Hall of Fame in 1957.

Crawford was not aware of the role Cobb played until after Ty died in 1961.[49]

---

[48] Crawford recounted this for Lawrence Ritter in *The Glory of their Times* years later.
[49] Bak, *Peach*, 176

Quotes about Cobb: Grantland Rice, one of the premier sports writers during Cobb's playing days, and one of Ty's closest friends in the media described Ty "as a cross between a tidal wave, cyclone and earthquake-fire wind and water all out on a lark; than out from the reel comes the glitter of steel, plus ten tons of dynamite hitched to a spark."

CHAPTER SIXTEEN
Cobb's Final Years With the Philadelphia Athletics

Cobb quotes:
"I find little comfort in the popular picture of me as a spike-slashing demon of the diamond, with a wild streak of cruelty in my nature. The fights and feuds I was to have engaged in have been steadily slanted to put me in the wrong. My critics have had their innings; I will have mine, now."

Rumors roamed around Detroit that after playing twenty-two years with the Tigers, Ty Cobb was set to hang up his spikes after the 1926 season, that this was his last year, and that he was planning to retire. Cobb squashed the rumors by telling reporters that he promised Connie Mack that he would fulfill his word and he intended to do so - and he did.

Cobb told reporters after the 1926 season that he would retire, but Mack persuaded him to, "Give it one more year." Ty, despite being 40 that year, batted .339 in 79 games.

Ty spoke to the press saying, "1927 would be my 22nd year in the game. I was tired and weary of traveling and being away from my family. I am concerned about breaking my legs - money is not the object. I am a man of my word, and I will honor my pledge to Connie. I am willing to take the chance that I will fine." he said.

Being a shrewd businessman, Connie was aware that having signed Tris Speaker and Cobb, two future Hall of Famers, two ex-managers, two super stars, and the possibility of getting into the World Series would appeal to both men.

In addition, this would excite the fans, increase attendance and possibly win the pennant. Connie saw this as a win-win for all.

The two aging stars both had fine seasons. Ty, forty, hit .357 in 123 games. Speaker, thirty-nine, hit .327 in 141 games. The rebuilding A's finished second 19 games behind one of the greatest teams in baseball. Led by Ruth and Lou Gehrig, the Yankees won 110 games and swept the Pittsburgh Pirates in the World Series, 4-0

Ty decided to give it one more year returning to Philadelphia in 1928 batting .323 and stealing six bases. Cobb had stolen home 53 times prior to a game on June 15th against the Cleveland Indians. He stole home that day for the 54th and final time of his career. He was never thrown out on any attempt to steal home.

Cobb was 41, a time when most players were well beyond their ability to play the game at the top of their ability but Cobb hadn't mellowed a bit.

The Georgia Peach's sixth summer as the club's player-manager had not been a successful one. Cobb had hit well enough; his .339 average stood out, but he was no longer an everyday player. He appeared in only 79 games, and in the second half of the season he'd reduced himself to a mostly pinch-hitting role. After July 5, he wrote his own name in the starting lineup only once, an August 20 game at Shibe Park against the Athletics, in which he collected three hits.

The St. Louis Browns, Washington Senators, Brooklyn Dodgers, and New York Giants all expressed an interest in Cobb, who, despite his age, was still a marketable commodity. But in the end, the Georgia Peach packed up his bat and glove and headed to the least likely metropolis in the American League, the city where he'd been vilified, denigrated, slandered, maligned, pilloried, abused, and even threatened by rooftop snipers. Philadelphia, the City of Brotherly Love.

On February 9, 1927, The Georgia Peach signed a one-year contract with Philadelphia at a salary of $40,000. He received a signing bonus of $25,000 and would collect an additional $10,000 at the end of the season.

Cobb knew that Connie was building, piece by piece, a baseball dynasty, a team that would enable Ty to make his dream of playing in the World Series come to fruition.

Cobb achieved his 4,000 career hit mark in 1927. Ironically, it came in a July 18 game against the Tigers at Navin Field.

Although the Athletics won 91 games in 1927, they were no match for Babe Ruth and the New York Yankees, considered by many baseball experts the greatest team of all time. The Yankees finished with 110 wins, a full 19 games ahead of the A's.

As for Cobb, he had a fine season, proving to the world that he could still play at a high level. In 133 games, he hit .357 with 93 RBIs. He topped the Athletics in hits with 175, runs scored with 104, and stolen bases with 22. Not bad for a 40-year-old man.

For the first half of 1928, Cobb was as productive as ever. But on July 26, in a game at Chicago's Comiskey Park, he was hit in the ribs by a pitch. X-rays proved negative, but the pain lingered, affecting his swing and mobility. At the time, Cobb was hitting .328. For the remainder of the season, he was relegated to pinch-hitting duties.

Cobb ended his baseball career with the Philadelphia Athletics near the end of the 1928 season. He certainly did not need the money as he was now a millionaire. He was forty-two, tired of playing baseball and concerned about injuring his body.

In his final game against the New York Yankees in Yankee Stadium on September 11th, he popped up to the shortstop in his last at-bat. He told Connie after the game, "If a man can't hit better than .323, he should hang up his spikes and glove." And that is what he did.

Cobb retired one year before the Athletics went to the World Series in 1929 beating the Chicago Cubs, 4-1.

In 1936, Cobb became the first player elected into the new Hall of Fame in Cooperstown, New York. Tris Speaker was inducted in 1937.

Despite all his talk of being weary of playing, tired of the traveling, being away from his family, his children and just plain wore out, he decided after the season to go to Japan and play ball there.

Ty Cobb in Japan 1928

As soon as the 1928 season ended, Cobb returned to his home in Augusta, Georgia and confirmed rumors in the local press that he was planning to go to Japan with other Major League players to play against various Japanese teams. Cobb sailed on October 24 to Japan but he was the only big league player to go. Also attending were his young children, Jimmy, Beverly and Herschel. The co-owner of the San Francisco Seals in the Pacific Coast League, a Mr. G.H. Putnam joined Ty and the children.

Cobb wore four different uniforms playing for four university teams: Keio, Waseda, Meiji and Osaka. He played mostly first base, and pitched some. Crowds up to 20,000 showed up for the ten exhibition games played. He also enjoyed coaching the youngsters. The four institutions and a Japanese newspaper sponsored the trip.

Cobb was head and shoulders over most of players in height and in playing ability. He wore a pre-World War II uniform with the name "Tokyo" emblazoned on his chest. The purpose of the Goodwill Visit to Japan was to help coach local teams, spread the sport of baseball and to show America's friendship with the Japanese.

The family returned by way of China, Manila and Honolulu arriving in San Francisco in time to celebrate Christmas in the City by the Bay. Ty spent Christmas with his family in Augusta answering reporters' questions about his plans for 1929. They were convinced he would play one more year in Philadelphia.

Cobb answered reporters' questions loudly and clearly stating, "I am going to retire while I am still The Georgia Peach - not a has-been, and I mean it."[50]

Unusual facts about Cobb: He was the first ball player to star in a movie, a drama by Grantland Rice, "Somewhere in Georgia."

---

[50] Rhodes, *Ty Cobb: Safe At Home.*

CHAPTER SEVENTEEN
Cobb and Rogers Hornsby

Cobb quotes:
"Don't ever give up. Don't be a quitter. Play the game to the limit from the time you start, till the last man is called out in the last inning."

Rogers Hornsby, Sr., nicknamed "The Rajah," was an infielder, manager, and coach who played 23 big-league seasons for six different teams and managed six teams. His St. Louis Cardinals won the World Series in 1926 against the New York Yankees.

Although Cobb is considered the greatest hitter in baseball, one cannot overlook the second best hitter, Rogers Hornsby, whose .358-lifetime average is second to Cobb and well ahead of such all-time greats as Tris Speaker (.345), Ted Williams (.344), Babe Ruth (.342), Lou Gehrig (.340), and Stan Musial (.331). Cobb batted left-handed; Hornsby batted from the right side making him the greatest right-handed hitter of all time. He won seven batting titles and led in home runs twice, 1922 and 1925.

His seven batting titles is, a feat tied or exceeded by only five players Cobb 12, Tony Gwynn (8), Honus Wagner (8), Rod Carew (7), and Stan Musial (7).

His batting average for the 1924 season was .424, a mark that no player has matched since. He was elected to the Hall of Fame in 1942 and the St. Louis Cardinals Hall of Fame in 2014.

Off the field, Hornsby was tough, uncompromising and outspoken. He was known as someone who was difficult to get along with, and he was not well liked by his fellow players, a major reason he changed teams so frequently in the last decade of his career. He usually left due to falling out with the front office. Most of the players he managed did not like him due to his insistence that others follow his lifestyle. On the field, he was the greatest right-handed batter in baseball history.

In 1924, Rogers Hornsby batted .424, yet failed to win the MVP. Hornsby led the league in batting average seven times, and led the league in nearly every other category at least once. He got going once the Deadball Era ended. 1920 was the first year he started looking like the elite hitter he became. Hornsby finished his career somehow missing out on 3,000 hits. His 1922 and 1924 seasons are considered two of the best in league history.

He also won the National League batting title seven times and hit over .400 three times including .424 in 1924. That is the best single season batting average in modern baseball history. It eclipsed the previous record of .420 held by Cobb since 1911.

Unlike Cobb, The Rajah as he was called could hit for power and led the league in home runs with 42 in 1922 and 39 in 1925.

In 1925, the year after he batted .424, he signed a three-year deal with the St. Louis Cardinals for $100.000, behind only Babe Ruth and Ty Cobb.

"Me and Roger played in different leagues so we didn't see each other during the season. I called him Rajah, he called me Peach," Cobb said.

Ty maintained: "He was tough and outspoken. He was a player-manager like me, and like me and other great hitters who became manager, he had a difficult time with players that were not as good as we were."

For example: Ted Williams was probably the smartest hitter to ever play professional baseball. But, as a manager for the Washington Senators, Teddy would routinely get angry at his player's inability to do things he did. "Why couldn't they see that pitch was four inches off the damn plate? How come they didn't *know* a change-up was coming?" Ted groaned to a reporter.

Cobb expressed his thoughts on the subject when he told a reporter who asked why great hitters fail at managing. He said, "Great players have a different experience when they played the game than a lousy player has. I understood success, while a lousy player understands struggle and failure. I had a gift that carried me during the years I played. A lousy player has to work hard and learn to play the game." Ty observed.

He continued, "We both managed, but I thought he was better than me because he managed the 1926 Cardinals to a World Series victory over the New York Yankees," Cobb noted.

Roger managed six different teams between 1925 and 1952.[51] Due to his volatile personality and difficulty getting along with the owners and his players, he was often fired.

---

[51] Cardinals, Giants, Braves, Cubs, Browns and Reds.

Hornsby was accused of being a KKK member that he vociferously denied. He was born in Winters, Texas, in 1896, and was often accused of being anti-Semitic and being a racist. He also denied these accusations.

Cobb was a guest of Hornsby during the classic game seven of the 1926 World Series against the New York Yankees. Roger always maintained winning the World Series was the highlight of his life.

The Series was tied three games each. The veteran, Grover Cleveland (Old Pete) Alexander pitched a complete game beating the Yankees 6-2 in game two.[52] He started and completed game 6 winning 10-1.

Alexander was a heavy drinker, and celebrated his game six win partying with friends until early in the morning, but he told Hornsby he would be ready in game seven if he was needed.

The Cardinals were leading 3-2 in the bottom of the seventh inning. The Yankees loaded the bases with two out and Hornsby brought in Old Pete to face Tony Lazzeri and struck him out.[53] Alexander's heroics preserved the Cardinals' Series-clinching win by a score of 3-2.

He retired the side in the bottom of the eighth and nailed the first two Yanks in the bottom of the ninth. Babe Ruth, who had already hit four home runs in the series, came to the plate to

[52] Grover Cleveland Alexander, nicknamed "Old Pete," was a pitcher who played from 1911 through 1930 for the Philadelphia Phillies, Chicago Cubs, and St. Louis Cardinals. Alexander's 90 shutouts are a National League record and his 373 wins are tied with Christy Mathewson for first in the National League record book.
[53] Anthony Michael Lazzeri was a second baseman during the 1920s and 1930s, predominantly with the New York Yankees. He was inducted into the Hall of Fame in 1991.

face an exhausted and dog-tired Alexander, who promptly walked Ruth.

On the first pitch to the next batter, Ruth dashed for second and was thrown out on a perfect throw to Hornsby who was playing at second.

After the game, Cobb asked Roger, "What did you ask Ruth after he slid in?"

Roger told Ty, "I asked Ruth what was he thinking? Ruth said nothing. He never looked at me - he picked himself up, and walked off the field."[54]

Lefty O'Doul, Ambassador to Japan

Lefty O'Doul, the fourth best hitter All-Time became known as the American Ambassador of Baseball to Japan. He first visited Japan in 1934 with Babe Ruth, Lou Gehrig, Jimmie Foxx, Lefty Grove, Charlie Gehringer, Al Simmons, Lefty Gomez, Connie Mack, Moe Berg and others.[55]

They travelled to Japan 1931 with an all-star team consisting of; Lou Gehrig, Al Simmons, Lefty Grove and many others. Many of the players were baffled as to why Berg was on the

---

[54] The seven highest lifetime batting average in MLB all time: Cobb .367 – Hornsby .358 J. Jackson .356 – Lefty O'Doul .349 – Tris Speaker .344 – Ted Williams .344 – Babe Ruth .342.

[55] Moe Berg was a United States spy, working undercover with the CIA. (It was not called CIA at that time) Moe spoke 15 languages - including Japanese. He had two loves: baseball and spying. In Tokyo, he ascended the tallest building in the city and filmed key features: the harbor, military installations, railway yards, etc. Eight years later, General Jimmy Doolittle studied Berg's films in planning his spectacular raid on Tokyo. After the war, Moe Berg was awarded the Medal of Freedom, America's highest honor for a civilian in wartime. After his death, his sister accepted the Medal. It now hangs in the Baseball Hall of Fame, in Cooperstown. The Presidential Medal of Freedom is the highest award given to civilians during wartime. Moe Berg's baseball card is the only card on display at the CIA Headquarters in Washington, DC.

roster due to his low batting average and clearly not an All Star. Lefty was injured about halfway through the tour so that gave him time to travel and get to know the people a little bit more.

Lefty was a gregarious person who enjoyed teaching probably above anything, even more than managing or playing. He enjoyed coaching players, and they were truly receptive to that. He immediately made plans to return in 1932 and coach the college players.

The Japanese wanted Babe Ruth to come to Japan for fifteen years but they couldn't get him to do it. Lefty O'Doul finally convinced Ruth to come. That tour was one of the major events in Japanese baseball history. It was the main reason that Lefty stayed behind and helped form professional baseball in Japan.

When O'Doul and many baseball greats like Babe Ruth, Lou Gehrig and others returned to baseball-crazy Japan in 1934, some fans wondered why a third-string catcher named Moe Berg was included. Although he played with five major-league teams from 1923 to 1939, he was a very mediocre ballplayer.

The visiting team won 17 straight games including 1-0 over teenager Eiji Sawamura, who whiffed Ruth, Gehrig, Foxx, and Gehringer in a row.

The Japanese were building their military in the mid-thirties. Cobb, not trusting the Japanese allegedly said, "Sometime in the near future, they may attack us, and we will have to fight them to the death."

The Empire of Japan attacked the Republic of China in 1937 and fought there until 1945. On December 7, 1941, Japan attacked Pearl Harbor in Hawaii drawing the United States into World War II. "A date that will live in infamy," President Franklin D. Roosevelt said.

Lefty returned after the war with his San Francisco Seals in 1949, and again in 1951 with an all-star squad including Joe DiMaggio, who hit the last home run of his career on the tour.

Cobb Quotes: "I always admired Connie Mack as a great Manager and a developer of hitters. He is a student of hitter and can discover their weaknesses and point them out with infallible accuracy. Star hitters cannot be made but a man with possibilities can be made under a teacher like Connie."

Cobb Statistics:

Most At Bats – Lifetime	11,429
Most Extra Base Hits – Lifetime	1,139
Most Singles – Lifetime	3,052
Most Years Batting Over .320	23

CHAPTER EIGHTEEN
Ty Cobb in Cuba

Cobb quotes:
"The base itself, for instance, often wasn't strapped down tight. The writers used to mention my "superstitious" habit of kicking the bag after I'd arrived at a base. Others thought it a nervous habit. What they didn't know was that with each kick, I moved that bag a few inches closer to me, after I'd taken my lead. If I had to dive back, that inch or two could be the difference. Never overlook the smallest percentages.

In late November 1910, the Detroit Tigers travelled to Havana, Cuba to play a series of exhibition games against an All Star team of the best players in Cuba.

On November 28 in Havana, with Luis González on the mound, the Cuban team defeated the Tigers 3-0.

Cobb arrived late as his Tigers had already played seven games winning 3, losing 3. One game ended in a tie due to a rain delay. The game was resumed, but due to poor lighting, the game was stopped.

Once Cobb arrived, the Tigers won four of five games, and became the first major league team to win a series in Cuba since

Brooklyn swept its four games in 1900. A Cuban sports writer wrote, "Taken all in all, the Detroit bunch is going away well pleased" (La Lucha, December 6, 1910).

Cobb had some base-stealing troubles in the series, specifically the November 28 loss to the Havana team. In that game, Cobb tried to bunt his way on with two outs in the first, but a Havana player pounced on the ball and tossed him out. In the fourth inning, Cobb walked and was again cut him down at second. In his other two plate appearances he rolled out to the pitcher, Luis González, and popped up to second baseman Home Run Johnson.

La Lucha, the Havana newspaper printed accounts for three of Cobb's five games. In those games, the only other incident on the base paths involving Cobb occurred on November 27. In that game against Almendares, Cobb tried to score from first on a hit by Sam Crawford, but was thrown out at home.

In a 3-2 Tigers win over Almendares on December 1, Cobb went 1 for 5. In the Tigers' 12-4 trouncing of Habana on December 4, Cobb went 2 for 5 with three runs scored. If Cobb tried to steal in these games, there is no indication of it in any Cuban papers.[56]

Major League Teams Play in Cuba

On May 3 1999, the Baltimore Orioles played an exhibition game against the Cuban national baseball team in Havana. This game marked the first time the Cuban national team had faced a squad composed solely of major league players and the first time an MLB team played in Cuba since 1959.

[5656] Aside from The Baseball Chronology, which was originally published in 1991, the earliest English-language source for this story is Michael and Mary Oleksak's El Béisbol: Latin Americans and the Grand Old Game , published in the same year. (p. 21) Reports of the Cobb games in Havana were reported in El Diario de la Marina or La Lucha (including the English-language papers).

Ever since President Barrack Obama opened an American Embassy in Havana, negotiations started with Cuba to normalize relations.

Several American and Cuban baseball sportsmen have begun discussions to bring an American Triple A Minor League team to Havana.

There are many obstacles in their path, but they are confident their dream will come to pass in the near future.

The Brooklyn Dodgers usually trained in Vero Beach, Florida during spring training. Jackie Robinson joined the team in 1947, becoming the first African-American to play in the Major Leagues. City ordinances in Vero Beach, Florida where the Dodgers normally trained prevented black and white players from competing on the same field against each other. To avoid problems caused by the segregated state of Florida, Dodger management decided the team would train in the Cuban capital of Havana. The Cuban people welcomed Jackie and the Dodgers with open arms

Players other than Cobb who have played in Cuba are: Babe Ruth, Ted Williams and Frank Robinson.

Quotes about Cobb: "He didn't outhit the opposition and he didn't outrun them, he out-thought them!" – Hall of Famer Sam Crawford

Cobb statistical records: Runs Batted in 1937 (Ranks 7th) 159

Little known facts about Cobb: Ty's favorite ice cream: Vanilla, peach (second choice) followed by chocolate, but seldom strawberry. Herschel Cobb Jr., Ty's grandson.

CHAPTER NINETEEN
Hall of Fame – Cobb Chosen First

Cobb quotes:
"I never could stand losing. Second place didn't interest me. I had a fire in my belly."

I t was mid-depression 1935, and business around the country had failed. People were looking for ways to improve this financial status, including in cities like Cooperstown, New York.

A group of local businessmen created the Clark Foundation, and sought to revive business and tourism after the Depression. Many baseball people believe that a Union Civil War Army officer Abner Doubleday, a Cooperstown native, had invented baseball in 1839. The group lobbied for a new museum dedicated to baseball to be built in Cooperstown. Though the Doubleday story was later discredited, the museum plans went ahead anyway.

The five charter Hall of Fame members were elected by members of the Baseball Writers' Association of America (BBWAA). The ballots revealed that five players had received at least 75 percent of the votes cast, setting a standard for admission to the Hall of Fame that still exists today.

On January 29, 1936 in Cooperstown, New York, the Baseball Hall of Fame announced the election of five charter members: Ty Cobb, Babe Ruth, Honus Wagner, Christy Mathewson and Walter Johnson.

Ty Cobb, an astoundingly productive hitter who won nine consecutive American League batting titles from 1907 to 1915, and twelve over his career received the most votes, appearing on 222 of the 226 ballots cast. Tying for second with 215 votes were Ruth, an ace left-handed pitcher for the Boston Red Sox who had smashed the league's home run records, and Honus Wagner, a star shortstop for the Pittsburgh Pirates who won eight National League batting titles and retired with more than 3,000 hits.

Christy Mathewson, New York Giants who pitched more winning games than any NL pitcher in history, received 205 votes, while Walter Johnson, Washington Senators one of the game's most powerful pitchers and career record holder for most strikeouts at the time of his retirement, received 189.

Ty Cobb's records

Ty Cobb was one of the best hitters to ever play Major League Baseball. At least that is what many baseball experts say. Look at the statistics that he put up during his 24-season professional career: .367 average (1st all time), 2246 runs scored (2nd all time), 4191 hits (2nd all time), 723 doubles (4th all time), 297 triples (2nd all time), 1938 RBI (6th all time), and 892 stolen bases (4th all time). He hit over 400 three times.

Ty Cobb and his amazing career have been discussed at length in this book, I wrote about his .367 career batting average and his induction into the MLB Hall of Fame in 1936. He hit over .300 each year in his baseball career from 1906 to 1928, including 21 years with the Detroit Tigers and the last two years with the Philadelphia Athletics.

Upper left: Honus Wagner, Pittsburgh Pirates
Upper right: Walter Johnson, Washington Senators
Front Row: Second from left: Babe Ruth, New York Yankees
Ty Cobb, Elected first place, failed to show.
Christy Mathewson, Died October 7, 1926.

The only year that Cobb didn't hit over .300 was in 1905, his rookie year with the Tigers; he hit .240. He became an everyday player the next season, he never had another season where he struggled and hit under .300.

His streak of twenty-two consecutive years hitting over .300 is a record that will never be broken. He hit over .320 in 22 different seasons (which is also a record).

His best year was 1911 when he led the league in runs, hits, triples, doubles, RBI, stolen bases, batting average, slugging percentage, and OPS.

His thinking part of the game, "brains as well as brawn," to quote him, is what separated him from everyone else. There are no films showing his ability to upset teams with his "harem scarem" base running, and his ability to get into the heads of his opponents. His psychological warfare was employed in getting other players to think or guess what he was going to do.

Ty had the ability to take the game to another level. He is comparable to a few modern ballplayers who used a similar approach. Jackie Robinson, Rickey Henderson and Pete Rose come to mind.

On September 11, 1985, Pete Rose broke Ty Cobb's hits record with his 4,192nd hit. His aggressive, over-the-top way he played the game is a man Cobb would have admired.

Although Pete Rose broke Ty's hit record, Major League Baseball might despise Pete Rose, but the former Cincinnati Red is still considered one of the most prolific hitters of all-time. Joining the 3,000 hit Club is considered an unbelievable accomplishment, and a surefire way to the Hall of Fame, but 4,000 is something that just doesn't happen in today's day and age. Rose's record is as safe as any in sports. Pete Rose is not in the Hall of Fame.

Ty Offers Advice and Opinions on Today's Game

There is a tendency on the part of old-timers to say the game and the players were better when they played the game. Cobb, out of baseball since he retired at the end of 1928, did not miss the game, but missed being talked about. He feared that in time, people would forget about him.

He enjoyed giving advice to young players like Joe DiMaggio, suggesting he use a lighter bat during the dog days of August, and not take fielding practice in the outfield during the hot August days, "It would wear you out" Ty would say.

Cobb admired the young Ted Williams and gave him some friendly advice but the hard hitting, upper swinging Ted was not too impressed with the dead ball singles hitting Ty's advice.

Ty had no connection to Major or Minor League baseball and his approach, and his thoughts on the game in the forties and fifties seemed to the modern ballplayers old-fashioned, and as extinct as a dodo bird. Modern hitters paid respect, and were in awe of what Cobb had accomplished, but the game Ty played as far as modern players were concerned was as dead as the Deadball was.

Ty did not offer advice to Stan Musial, who Ty thought was the perfect hitter.

The Game has Changed

Cobb played in the Deadball Era, 1905-1920. Between the mid-forties and throughout the fifties, Ty's comments on the game made him seem out of touch with the stars and players of the time. I don't think he appreciated how the game had changed: the players are bigger, stronger, faster and smarter than the old-timers, and they throw the ball faster, hit it harder and fielded it better. There are thirty-two teams, designated hitters in one league, instant replay, and despite night games and national travel, modern players are better. Another big change is the use of a bullpen that consists of young studs who threw 95 to 100 mph.

Five man starting staffs, pitch counts, pitchers not finishing what they started. There were too many home runs and high-scoring games. All things the fans love. A 1-0 game is a rarity to be appreciated by baseball aficionados.

Yet the game has never been more popular. Attendance has never been higher. Some games are played outside the USA. Starting in 1996, The San Diego Padres played the New York Mets in Monterrey, Mexico and Japan. In 2000, the Chicago Cubs played the Mets in Tokyo, Japan. In 2014, The Dodgers played the Arizona Diamondbacks in Sydney, Australia. Some teams played in San Juan, Puerto Rico. Europe is not far behind. Cuba is being considered.

There were eight teams when Ty played, there are now thirty-two. The game stopped as far west as St. Louis, and teams traveled by train. Now there are teams in California and Florida. There were two teams in Canada, now one. Teams moved from city to city, Philadelphia Athletics to Kansas City, then Oakland. Boston Braves moved from Boston to Milwaukee in 1953. Then Atlanta. The Dodgers and Giants went west to California. The Reserve Clause was the rule when Cobb played, then came free agency, agents and out of sight salaries. Then came Jackie Robinson, and all the great African-American players that Cobb never had to play against.

Only two players, Babe Ruth and Roger Maris hit 60 home runs. Before 1960, only 9 players hit over 50 home runs. Since 1960, twenty players have hit over 50, several twice. Two hit over 70, Barry Bonds and Mark McGuire. Blame it on steroids, too many teams, and too many pitchers who would never have played the show when there were only eight teams. Perhaps they were better athletes?

There are three eternal truths about baseball. They are said today, and they were said as far back as the early 20th century: "Baseball has become too much a business. Nobody knows how to bunt today. Today's pitchers are wimps compared to the old days. Today's pitchers are better than the old-timer, but they never finish what they start. There are more worn-out shoulders than ever. Thank God for Tommy John surgery.

Also: every person believes that baseball, music and sex were better back when they were between the ages of 16-30. A fan told me, "I will never see a player better than Willie Mays, partly because he was among the very best, but also because he was the first player I saw who was among the best, but also because I saw things better then."

Some folk think that analytics in baseball are scientifically valid but make for less exciting games. And finally, there are all the new categories: GIDP, OBP, OPS, SBR, BFP, WAR, OBO, GOAO, IRA and BABIP (batting average on balls in play).

Cobb always believed the players he played with were better than the boys who played in the 40's or fifties. Ted Williams believed the players of the 50's, 60's and 70's were the best that ever played. Perhaps the players at the turn of the twenty-first century will believe that this bunch of professionals were the best that ever played the game.

Quotes about Cobb: "I pick Ty Cobb first for the Hall of Fame. I guess everyone will do the same." - Connie Mack, Owner and Manager, Philadelphia Athletics.

ABOUT THE AUTHOR
Norm Coleman

Norm's circuitous journey to a successful career as a writer and performer is as compelling as the character he portrays.

For over 30 years, Norm Coleman was an award-winning professional photographer. He operated a successful Photography studio in San Mateo, California, and travelled the world. His clients were among San Francisco's elite.

But times changed and Norm's world began to come apart. Eventually, he and his family became homeless, living in his car with two dogs and only the possessions they could cram in. Those were dark days indeed.

At age seventy, tired of roaming the desert of life as a lost soul, it was time for a change. Now, living alone in the bucolic seaside village of Half Moon Bay in Northern California, the fog of self doubt and despair started to lift and Norm began the slow process of rebuilding his life. There, in the unhurried pace of this coastal hamlet breathing fresh salt air, he discovered the comfort and meaning that religious experience can bring to one's existence.

One day, as stopped in a local spot for his morning coffee, Norm saw a notice that the local theater company was holding auditions for an upcoming production of "Inherit The Wind." Now open to new things, he stepped out of his comfort zone and auditioned. He got a part in the production and suddenly discovered the magic of performing before a live audience.

Combining his newfound interest in live performance and his lifelong love of baseball, Norm began working on a new project, a one-man show on the life of Ty (The Georgia Peach) Cobb. He poured his new creative energy into extensive research and the massive effort to create a script and mount the production. He brought Cobb to life in over 60 cities in Northern California while dreaming of taking his show on the road nationally.

Thanks to his friendship over the years with David Dombrowski, then CEO, President and General Manager of the Detroit Tigers,

Norm was able to perform for Tiger fans in Lakeland, Florida, the winter home of the Detroit Tigers. When not on stage, he spent hours making contacts and promoting his show. It paid off with performances at the Gerald R. Ford Presidential library in Grand Rapids, Michigan and at the request of the Cobb family, at the Ty Cobb Museum in Royston, Georgia.

From there, Norm went on to receive standing ovations in Boston; Detroit; Atlanta; Aiken, South Carolina; Jackson, Mississippi; Victoria, BC; Pasadena and San Francisco, California. Truly a life re-imagined for Norm Coleman, now in his mid seventies.

Still performing and writing at eighty-one, when asked what inspired him to take on this project twelve years ago, Norm said, "Ty Cobb was one of the greatest baseball players in history... the first player elected to the Baseball Hall of Fame. But personally, he was a very complicated individual, misunderstood and often maligned... the victim of myths and misinformation... but one of the most intriguing sports figures I have ever encountered. I needed a challenge to try something I had never done before. My goal was to debunk the myths and tell the truth by bringing Cobb to life so that audiences everywhere could see him for the man he was... the greatest Tiger of them All."

With determination, newfound confidence and lots of hard work, Norm has accomplished his goal. The reviews are in and his one man show has been called, "Entertaining, humorous, historical, a walk down memory lane for baseball fans and the story of American History at the turn of the Century."

At eighty-one, Norm Coleman is not planning to slow down anytime soon. For him, "Anything is possible regardless of your age."

18053721R00109

Printed in Great Britain
by Amazon